A Life Inspired
Tales of Peace Corps Service

Peace Corps
Paul D. Coverdell Peace Corps Headquarters
1111 20th Street, NW
Washington, D.C. 20526

www.peacecorps.gov
800.424.8580

A Life Inspired: Tales of Peace Corps Service

September 2008 • Library of Congress Catalog No. 2008929102

ISBN 9780964447288

Use of Peace Corps Name and Logo

Contents

Foreword

Living a Life Inspired
Ron Tschetter

Making a Difference

A Life Changing Experience
Ron and Nancy Tschetter · India 3

My Moroccan Brother
Mark Huffman · Morocco 11

Thinking Beyond Borders
Steve Biedermann · Kiribati 15

Angel
Barbara Arrington · South Africa 21

¿Ya Ves? (Do you See It Now?)
Paul Ruesch · Mexico 25

Talking of Trees
Aaron Welch · Domincan Republic 31

The Faces of an Acacia Tree
Karin Vermilye · Cameroon 35

Women Can Learn Things, Too
Amber B. Davis-Collins · Honduras 41

The Work Continues 45
Kelly Daniel · Kenya

Cultural Understanding

Going the Distance 51
Curtis Blyden · Mongolia

Hope Dies Last 55
Patrick Burns · Moldova

Soybean Transformations 59
John Sheffy · Togo

Saying Goodbye 65
Caroline Chambre · Bukina Faso

Taking Time 69
Walter Hawkes · Tanzania

The Importance of Drinking Tea 75
Jake Jones · Morocco

Been There, Done That 79
Stephanie Saltzman · Zambia

Itam 83
Jeff Fearnside · Kazakhstan

Leave Taking 89
Beth Genovese · Panama

Window to the World

Harvesting Friendship 95
Kay Oursler · Tanzania

Enough Time 99
Diana Schmidt · Ukraine

If There's Enough for One 105
Kara Garbe · Burkina Faso

There is Time 111
Casey Laycock · Bulgaria

¡Que Milagro! 115
Kerrie A. Resendes • Guatemala

Hummingbirds or Fairies? 119
Megan Mentrek • Kyrgyzstan

Changing Perspectives 125
Christina Luongo • Bolivia

Different Kinds of Lessons in Moldova 129
April Simun • Moldova

The Train Ride Home 133
Robin Solomon • Kazakhstan

A Special Meal in Tunisia 137
Jody Olsen • Tunisia

Becoming a Peace Corps Volunteer

Becoming a Peace Corps Volunteer 145

Map: Countries Featured in the Stories 146

Foreword

Living "A Life Inspired"
Ron Tschetter · Director of the Peace Corps

A s Director of the Peace Corps, it has been my honor to have met Peace Corps Volunteers all over the world and to have seen firsthand the remarkable dedication, passion, and skill they bring to serving others. The work of Peace Corps Volunteers builds on a legacy that has become a significant part of America's history. In 1961, President John F. Kennedy called Americans to serve in the Peace Corps. Now, almost half a century later, more than 190,000 Americans have answered President Kennedy's call and have helped to improve the lives of millions of people around the world and at home.

My wife, Nancy, and I were Peace Corps Volunteers in India from 1966 to 1968. We were in our 20s, recent college graduates and newly-weds when we decided to serve in the Peace Corps. We spent two years living and working in India and learned to speak the local language. We came away from our experience with a great appreciation for the culture and values of the people of India.

Peace Corps Volunteers come from the diverse fabric that is America—people from all different cultural and ethnic backgrounds—young people in their 20s to Volunteers age 50 and above. Nearly 8,000 Peace Corps Volunteers are currently working throughout the world in the areas of education; youth and community development; health and HIV/AIDS awareness; business development; information communication and technology; environment; and agriculture.

The Peace Corps prepares Volunteers with extensive language, technical, and cross-cultural awareness training. Volunteers also share their unique perspectives on America with their friends and colleagues overseas, and when they return home, they bring not only valuable real-world skills for future endeavors, but also an expanded worldview to share with their fellow Americans.

As you will see from our collection of stories, even for the best-prepared Volunteer there are still surprises. There are also highs, lows, and flashes of insight gained through the Peace Corps experience. Volunteers come away with a greater understanding of the world and a feeling their lives have been deeply enriched.

Through their stories, our lives become enriched as well. A world of insight, this book is a brief sampling of what it means to have served as a Peace Corps Volunteer and to have experienced a life inspired.

Making *a Difference*

A Life Changing Experience
Ron and Nancy Tschetter · India

Ron: You can't imagine what an honor it is for me to serve as Director of the Peace Corps, whose noble mission is to promote peace and friendship worldwide. It brings full circle the journey my wife, Nancy, and I began in 1966, serving as Volunteers in India. The spirit of compassion and giving that our parents passed on to us growing up in South Dakota and Minnesota is a big part of what led us to join the Peace Corps. We were also intrigued by the idea of being totally immersed in a different culture and living in a very different place.

We were newlyweds when we entered the Peace Corps, having been married for about a year. We saw an ad on television that called the Peace Corps "The Toughest Job You'll Ever Love." We were both struck by that message, and we decided to sign up to serve as a couple.

Though it was many years ago, our Peace Corps experience still reverberates in our lives and the lives of those with whom we were honored to work. You see, once you do something so bold, so enriching, and so all-encompassing, you realize that volunteering and giving to others is actually a gift to yourself. Our lives, and certainly our perspectives, were changed forever.

Nancy: The Peace Corps was a bit different back then—nowadays Volunteers do their training in-country to become familiar with the culture and language, but back then our training was held in the U.S., and we

> *Our lives, and certainly our perspectives, were changed forever.*

were sent overseas when it was time to begin our assignment. We completed our training on December 15, and, after an evening out and one last dinner in New York City, we left the Big Apple on a plane bound for London and the great beyond.

The following evening we boarded an Air India charter, a Boeing 707 full of anxious Peace Corps Volunteers just like ourselves. We flew all night to Delhi, India. I will never forget when we arrived, stepping off the plane: the smoky haze that rose from hundreds of small brown huts; the exotic smell of dinner prepared over wood fires; the pungent, tropical air. We were truly on the other side of the world in a culture very different from our own.

We traveled on to Bombay as a group. We assumed the Volunteers would all stay together to celebrate Christmas, but that wasn't the case—we were sent right to our sites. Within a heartbeat of our arrival it seemed, we received our train tickets and were told, "Ron and Nancy, you're going to Parbani." We were actually being sent to a village 18 miles beyond Parbani, but we didn't know it at the time. Late in the evening on Christmas Eve, we took a train with half a dozen other Volunteers who would be getting off at different points. Ron and I were the last Volunteers on board when we arrived at the Parbani railhead at about 9:30 p.m. We were met by Shri Baraswedker, our new co-worker. The rail station canteen was closed, but Bara thought we'd be hungry so he found a cook to make us an omelet for our dinner. Our journey wasn't over yet—we still had to go a good 45 minutes by Jeep in the cool night air to get to our final destination, Bori village.

It was midnight when we finally arrived at our new community. Undeterred by the late hour, our proud host gave us a short tour of the village, including the centerpiece of local entertainment, an outdoor movie theater that was currently in full gear, loud music blaring.

Decades later, I can still recall our exhaustion when we finally arrived at our house. It was situated among a block of shops, all resembling one another. Here, traders would sell their wares from the ground floor and live upstairs on the second floor.

Bara found us some plain metal bed frames, on loan from the clinic until we got our own, and we threw our sleeping bags on the frames and fell right to sleep. We didn't even realize we had a bedroom on the second floor until the next day! Things were very basic. We had a tank that we would fill with water, and a "basket latrine" inside the house. A little balcony upstairs added a touch of luxury.

In the morning we were awakened by a loud rumbling sound. We were sure something was coming right through our door because our windows and door were closed. Now, in daylight, we saw that we were located right on the street front, and that the noise was the bullock carts rolling by. That's how we woke up every morning.

The day began with greetings from a neighboring shopkeeper, who stopped by to wish us a Merry Christmas. We spent Christmas Day shopping for needed supplies. We had received an allowance from Peace Corps, and set to remedy our empty cupboards. We went to the market and bought some cooking utensils. Then we looked for food that we could recognize from our lives on the farm—eggplant, onions, eggs. We also found bread, shortbread cookies, and some instant coffee. We ended up making ourselves a fine omelet that evening for our Christmas feast.

Ron: We gradually became acquainted with our environment. India, at that time, still revolved around a caste system, and we lived among the people we were to serve; they were called "untouchables." These were people from the lowest caste in Indian society, and they were very, very poor. Together with our Indian counterparts, we worked in a community health center at the other end of the village about a quarter of a mile away. We came to know our neighbors by walking to and from the clinic. From assisting in the clinic and living in our local community, we quickly learned about the development problems related to rural health. Certain illnesses such as dysentery, cholera, and malaria took their toll, and children were subject to catching every sort of childhood disease. Epidemics such as smallpox and cholera could wreak havoc on a population already struggling.

I remember one day when a Jeep stopped and beeped in front of our house—it was the local sanitary inspector, one of my colleagues, and a few regional health workers. The inspector told me to get in, that we were going to a nearby village. He didn't explain why, but merely told me that it was an emergency situation. When we got to the village, I saw that it was a nomadic community called Lamanis that had been ravaged by smallpox. The families had come to that spot down by a river to let their animals graze, and they were living in small thatched-roofed huts.

We spoke to the village leader and got his consent to distribute medicine. Every hut had victims, and people all around us were dying of smallpox. The stench was unbearable. Not everyone took the medicine we gave them since many didn't believe it would cure them. The word for smallpox in their language translated to "God's will," and most of the nomadic community believed that to be true. It was heartbreaking to see. Many people died, but a lot of people survived. That experience left a great impression on me.

Nancy: Two young boys from a lower caste family who lived close by were in the habit of hanging out on our front porch. We gradually got to know them and their family quite well, and we became close friends. Eventually, in order to help out the boys and their family with a little extra income, we'd give the boys small jobs to do for us like fetching water or running to the open air market.

We were also able to help their father by giving him a microloan to open a small kiosk where he sold small drugstore items. Because of the microloan and the success of his kiosk, the family was eventually able to move to a bigger village and open a small store. The boys and their four brothers and sisters were also able to get through school, which was no small accomplishment for this family.

It was natural to wonder then how much of an impact we were

making in the face of such widespread poverty. We knew that our Peace Corps experience clearly expanded our horizons and taught us a great deal about how life is for people who are struggling in other parts of the world. We learned to appreciate what we have as Americans, and how as global citizens we have a responsibility to others

> *We learned to appreciate what we have as Americans, and how as global citizens we have a responsibility to others who are less fortunate.*

who are less fortunate. But was it really possible for two young people to make a difference? It may be simply that we influenced one person, or one family, or one village in a faraway place. However, the effect was no less significant, for those individuals were the people we had come to know and care about during our years of Peace Corps service.

We have been fortunate to go back to India five times and to have kept in contact with the family we knew so well. We do know that we impacted at least two people—the young boys who used to hang out on our doorstep. Both of them finished school and grew up to be successful businessmen, and each has three lovely children.

Interestingly enough, these young men were with us when we were working with the local community on birth spacing. We still keep in touch with one of them. He has since told us that he and his wife decided to have three children and no more, largely due to what we talked about way back then. He told us that he knew he would be better able to provide for a smaller sized family. Fortunately for him, that has proven true.

Ron: Since becoming Peace Corps Director, I have had the privilege of visiting 1,500 Volunteers in 42 countries from Botswana to Bolivia. I've seen that the challenges now are as great as they were back when Nancy and I served, or maybe even greater. I continue to be deeply impressed by the commitment of Peace Corps Volunteers.

In Namibia, I met Judith Harper, a 63-year-old educator working as a teacher trainer. The primary educators she assists accord Judith with a great deal of respect. Her expertise and life experiences are highly valued. Judy had wanted to join the Peace Corps for a long time, and even extended her service for an additional year.

I also saw Jason Sears in Namibia. A Volunteer from Idaho, Jason is working with his counterpart to teach students in a local high school to repair a storehouse full of broken computers. The next stage of his project, he told me, will be to place the newly operational computers in local schools, and to teach kids how to use them. Having learned a range of computer skills from Jason, his industrious students are using software to make photos of their classmates into gift cards they can sell.

In Mongolia, I spent the day with Sean Speer, a Volunteer working as an English language instructor at a rural village school. Sean lives in a *ger*, which is a type of nomadic hut that many Mongolians use. Although modernized with a refrigerator and even Internet access, life in a ger has its challenges, including an outhouse that requires a cold trek through the snow in the winter. By living in a style similar to the people he serves, Sean has forged a deep relationship with his local community. This is as appreciated, as are the English classes he teaches and the library he helped develop.

In Swaziland, I met Joe and Amy Mayer, a couple from North Dakota who are working on an HIV/AIDS prevention and treatment project. The Mayers live on a traditional chief's homestead and have helped build and operate a *KaGogo*, or "grandma's house," where HIV prevention, mitigation, and care activities take place in the community. People from the outlying villages can come and get food for those who are HIV-positive. Joe and Amy also help a support group work on income-generating ideas, counsel youth, and teach life skills to students at the high school and upper primary levels.

Nancy and I both feel that the Peace Corps continues to be an exciting, life-changing experience. We see incredible dedication among today's Volunteers, and salute the courage and optimism we see in so many of them. I truly enjoy leading this agency, which continues to set the gold standard for volunteerism. If you haven't yet looked into becoming a Peace Corps Volunteer, we both urge you to do so—there's no better time than now.

Ron Tschetter was nominated by President George W. Bush and confirmed by the United States Senate as the 17th Director of the Peace Corps on September 13, 2006. He and his wife, Nancy, served in India as community health Volunteers from 1966 to 1968. After returning to the United States, Mr. Tschetter enjoyed a long and distinguished career in the financial securities industry, and he chaired the board of the National Peace Corps Association.

Improving the lives of others has been a lifelong passion for both Ron and Nancy. After her Peace Corps service, Nancy worked as a social worker in Minnesota. They have two sons and, at last count, three grandchildren.

My Moroccan Brother

Mark Huffman · *Morocco*

"**F**in gadi temshi? Aji!"

"Where are you going? Come here!" I shouted over and over as Youssef made a complete turn and headed toward the wrong goal.

It was our first day of using a flag football kit the Chicago Bears had donated. Over 30 boys, ranging in age from 9 to 20, joined me at the town *souk*—an open market where fruits, vegetables, and various household wares are sold twice a week. On this particular day, we had the large, dusty field to ourselves and I decided to introduce the kids to a new sport.

Youssef proceeded to do a perfect impression of Roy "wrong way" Riegels, whose misdirected run in the 1929 Rose Bowl is considered by many to be the worst blunder in the history of college football.

A bit frustrated, but laughing at the same time, I decided that American football was too difficult to explain and adapted the rules a bit. The Peace Corps, I would learn, is a constant source of adapting—whether it be handwashing your clothes or eating a goat's brain directly from the skull as it sits on the kitchen table.

A middle-aged journalist who had endured few changes prior to joining the Peace Corps, I embraced the adventure that living in another country provided. Originally staying with a large Berber family, I learned to separate the Moroccan Arabic from the French and Tamazight my host father would combine into one sentence.

> *The Peace Corps,*
> *I would learn, is*
> *a constant source*
> *of adapting.*

I adjusted to the wild barking dogs and the roosters that didn't know the difference between midnight and 5 a.m. I also became accustomed, to the point of enjoying, the loud calls to prayer that would bellow from the mosques five times a day. Bartering for goods, fasting during Ramadan, and having the dead skin rubbed from my back at the public bathing house also became norms. I began to adopt routines, such as stopping at one of the neighborhood cafes to enjoy a glass of hot mint tea, where I got to know many people from my village.

I met Khalid Belhaj while teaching English at the youth center. Sitting among a small group of teens who would joke and shout out answers before raising their hands, he stood out because of his polite demeanor and strong willingness to learn. Khalid's attendance was sporadic that first winter due to a full schedule of classes at a university in Fes. The school was just 40 miles away, but travel difficulties required students to be housed there during the week.

Absorbing my rudimentary English lessons whenever he could break away from his studies, Khalid would eventually reveal his desire to become an English teacher. He was unable to find a job upon graduation that spring and I asked if he would like to get some practice by helping me at the youth center. Thus began a friendship.

Known in El Menzel, a town of about 9,000 people, for his ability to fix just about anything—from computers to broken bicycle chains— Khalid often takes on such duties without compensation and struggles to help support his family. He continues to search for work as a teacher, but contributes to his community in the meantime teaching French and tutoring youth.

Near the end of my first year of service, Khalid and I learned about a reformatory in Fes that housed boys from ages 8 to 18. Having been involved with at-risk youth before joining the Peace Corps, I thought this would be a great opportunity to help mentor the boys, who were incarcerated for everything from petty theft to murder. Initially attempting to teach English to the youth on a biweekly basis, we soon realized many of them had no real interest in learning the language but that through sports we could reach them. Thus, we launched a sports club, playing soccer or basketball on a regular basis.

I was able to mix my love of sports with mentoring and eventually approached Khalid and the center's director about a two-day camp. They embraced the idea and the first such venture in Morocco was launched. I recruited four fellow Peace Corps Volunteers and three students from a neighboring village and we spent a summer weekend that the participants will never forget. The kids enjoyed a variety of sports and games and earned medals for their accomplishments at the end of the camp. Soccer jerseys and shorts donated by the U.S. embassy also made their way to Fes that memorable weekend.

Khalid had hopes of continuing his involvement at the reformatory after I was gone and we had spoken about starting a mentoring program with a university that is just a short walk from the facility.

Khalid had also become known by the Peace Corps staff in Morocco due to his strong involvement in my community and even accompanied me for a pre-service training session where we talked to incoming Volunteers about identifying community resources.

A valuable working partner, Khalid and I would meet at a local café to go over lesson plans. Near the end of my service, our two-man English teaching team had become a one-man show, with Khalid being a far better teacher than myself. Away from the classroom, we often met for Moroccan mint tea and roasted peanuts or hot milk and coffee. A Muslim with somewhat conservative ideals, Khalid would ask about America's view of his religion. He noted that I was the first American he had gotten to know as a friend and, while we may not have shared all of the same ideals, we agreed that religion should never get in the way of friendship. "Too bad we can't get the world leaders to join us for tea at the café," he would joke.

One of those individuals who preferred to stay in the background, Khalid received few accolades for his work in El Menzel, yet he was at the forefront of much of the progress seen at the youth center during my two years there. I often had to nudge him to the front of the room as town officials and association members traded congratulatory handshakes whenever they had a large event at the center.

"I never would have done these things if it hadn't been for you," Khalid said during my last week in Morocco, bringing a lump to my throat as I realized the sustainability my program managers had emphasized so much had come to fruition. I had also gained a friendship that endures, despite being separated by nearly 4,000 miles.

As the 18th century English writer Samuel Richardson said, "A brother may not be a friend, but a friend will always be a brother."

Moving to Washington, D.C., four months after completing my Peace Corps service, I still find myself reflecting on such experiences. Just last week I couldn't help but smile when I heard a Moroccan man, Ridouane Harroufi, had won the annual Cherry Blossom Ten Mile Run in our nation's capital. He obviously ran the right way.

Mark Huffman served as a youth development Volunteer in Morocco from 2005 to 2007, joining the Peace Corps after a 20-year career in journalism. He taught English and led a variety of programs aimed toward youth development, including HIV/AIDS education and leadership camps. Mark became communications editor for the Peace Corps in Washington, D.C., in March of 2008.

Thinking Beyond Borders
Steve Biedermann · Kiribati

As the annual migration of wildebeest and zebra made their way across the Serengeti, I found myself on a two-week safari, vacationing in Kenya during the summer of 2001. It was a well needed hiatus from the stress of trading bonds on the capital markets desk of an American investment bank. After fifteen years of chasing bonuses, this trip was an opportunity to reflect on the desire to do more than make a living, perhaps to make a life. The need in Africa is obvious, and the waters of my soul were stirred to answer the call.

The vacation ended and a return to the comforts of an ordinary life included photo albums depicting the journey. Little did I realize that the journey had only begun.

A few months later, I sat on the trading desk early one morning, focusing on bids and offers, and life stopped as I watched the events of September 11, 2001, unfold before me. That evening over dinner and discussion of what had happened, two unpopular questions nagged at me: What role did we, as an American society, play in the tragedy of that day? And more importantly, What was I willing to do about it?

After investigating several options for international service work, the choice to serve in the Peace Corps became obvious as the best fit. A long track record of successful grass roots development work, only going where invited by the host country, and despite my own deep spiritual beliefs, the Peace Corps was a governmental agency with no particular religious

> *I slowly began to realize that the best chance I had for success was simply to start with the question: How can I help?*

affiliation. Throughout the application and interview process, I stressed that my desire to serve came from a longing to share my time, talents, and experience in order to build bridges across cultural lines.

I was invited to serve in western Russia and perform international business development work, with a departure scheduled for August of 2002. The Peace Corps always mentions that flexibility is a necessary attribute for any prospective volunteer, and so when I had already sold my home and cars, resigned from my job, put my belongings into a pre-paid storage unit, and purchased a duffel bag full of winter clothes; it should not have been a surprise when the Peace Corps recruiter called in early August to inform me that the program in Russia had just been terminated and they would need to find me a new assignment. It would have been easy to panic at this point, as I was walking away from everything my culture said to hold onto, but I knew sacrifice was part of the deal. The recruiter called the next day with an invitation to serve in the central Pacific island nation of Kiribati, departing in October; however, a specific area of work assignment was openly labeled as Community Development. I enthusiastically accepted, unpacked the winter clothes and repacked with flip-flops, shorts, and a lot of sunscreen.

What I needed to pack, most importantly, was a heart to truly serve others, which I would learn over and over again throughout the next two years.

The transition to Peace Corps service was anything but easy and I wanted to quit a thousand times, beginning with the first day of training. Coming from corporate America to an agency of the U.S. government, working in one of the most isolated countries of the world, was countercultural. I slowly began to realize that the best chance I had for success was simply to start with the question: How can I help? This basic query led to a post as a mathematics instructor at Teabike College on the remote outer island of Tabiteuea North. The college was a public boarding school where students in Forms 4, 5, and 6 came from all of the other islands of Kiribati for secondary school education. The greatest need was for an instructor to teach higher level math to the Form 6 students in order to prepare them for the Pacific Secondary School Certificate exams, which are taken annually for qualification to continue university education overseas. With no prior formal teaching experience, but a lifelong passion for mathematics, and a growing heart toward service, I became "Sir" to a classroom of several dozen teenagers. I solicited textbooks from the Australian high commissioner and solar powered calculators from my church in the States.

The students and I quickly discovered that laughter was the first and easiest bridge to cross in the cultural divide that existed between us. They saw that I came as a Volunteer interested in living as they did, in a stick hut, eating their simple meals of fish and rice, collecting rainwater to quench the equatorial heat, and embracing their rich culture. In exchange, I gave them calculus, statistics, differential equations, and a grassroots look at America through the heart of a man longing to make a difference in the world.

The challenges were many and at times appeared insurmountable. I had disconnected from the daily life of the Internet; cold, safe drinking water from the tap; the variety of plentiful food; a climate-controlled home; and familiar relationships with those I knew. I was on a small strip of coral with ocean to the left, and ocean to the right. I felt the isolation from my world back home passing by as time stood still on the equator, struggling to hold onto the relationships that mattered most. I continually faced the question as to whether I was really making a difference.

As the weeks turned to months and I began to willingly embrace the simple village life, I realized my attitude had changed. It was still the same small island, with the unbearable heat, the same meal of fish and rice daily, and all of the same internal struggles. What changed was the fact that I made peace with the truth that it was not about me or my comfort, it was about those teenagers in that classroom. The kids who started by calling me "sir," but eventually grew comfortable calling me Steven as they waited anxiously for math class to begin. The ones I grew to love and be loved by. The ones who write me e-mails today as they continue their studies at universities in other countries and thank me for challenging them to go further, to think beyond borders.

After completing my two years of service, I feel I am now a citizen of two countries, one that I was born into, and another of which I chose to give two years of my life. I frequently listen to a tape recording of my Teabike College students singing at my farewell party and it brings me back to that place—the small island of Tabiteuea North, where the equator intersects with the International Date Line, in the Republic of Kiribati, where I proudly served in the toughest job I ever will love.

The transition home to America was, in most ways, more difficult. I heard it once said that a man never steps into the same river twice. When people asked how it was being "home," I would respond by taking off my eyeglasses and telling them that before I left I think I looked at our culture "like this," and now that I am back I see it "like this," and I put my glasses back on. It is not that America was different, but more so that my perspective had transformed into a broader world view. Many asked if the Peace Corps experience changed me and, after thinking about it, I realized the experience helped define me. The opportunity to serve gave me clarity on what was truly important to me and crystallized where my values lay.

I decided to combine my years of finance experience with my new-found passion for making a difference in education. I accepted a position as the investment portfolio manager at Chicago Public Schools. It is truly a unique opportunity for me to make a daily difference in one of the nation's largest urban school districts and I consider it Peace Corps with a suit and tie. I'm serving as a board member with Thinking Beyond Borders, an international education organization that was cofounded by a fellow returned Peace Corps Volunteer from Kiribati. I also mentor two teenage boys from Sierra Leone who came to live in Chicago as refugees.

I was also able to serve as a United Nations volunteer for three months in Sudan after attending a UN conference on development in Africa. It was in Sudan that a friend passed along an interview from a doctor serving with Médecins Sans Frontières in the Darfur region. When asked why he served, the doctor commented, "You reach a certain age and you have to stop thinking about being the kind of man you want to be, and start being that man."

Steven Biedermann served as a mathematics education Volunteer in the Republic of Kiribati in the Central Pacific from 2002 to 2004. He taught at an outer island secondary school; cross trained teaching staff on generator-powered personal computers; and provided expertise in business development to microenterprise ventures. Upon his return to the United States, Steven went to work with the Chicago Public Schools Bureau of Treasury as an investment portfolio manager.

Angel

Barbara Arrington · South Africa

I awoke to the sounds of singing and the pounding of feet. The beautiful yet haunting sound of voices in harmony moved closer as men and women paraded down the red dirt road in a Saturday ceremony for the dead. AIDS was making its own inexorable march across my village of over 3,000 families, snatching someone away almost weekly. And while AIDS was talked about, few people accepted its existence among them. Those who had the disease were shunned.

One of those was a young woman who called herself Angel. When she was born, her mother named her Mankhu, which means death in Northern Sotho. In the end, she would use her life to be an example so that others could live.

My primary job as a Peace Corps Volunteer was to help teachers implement a new outcome-based curriculum adopted by the South African government in their schools. My secondary job was left up to me. Based on the needs of my community, I could decide what project outside of the school I wanted to do. As I sought the perfect fit, one came knocking at my door.

"Mabatu!" My host mother called out my South African name.

"Yebo, Ke etla!" (Yes, I'm coming!) I replied.

"You have a visitor," my host mother said at my door, coming to me instead.

Outside, under a large mango tree, sat a woman, neatly dressed in a

> *Though I am black like they are, I am still a stranger, so they are surprised that I can speak their language.*

white button-down blouse and navy blue skirt.

"*Dumelang,*" (hello) I said.

"*Aowa! O bolela!*" (No way! You are speaking my language!) she said, as many do when they hear me speak.

Though I am black like they are, I am still a stranger, so they are surprised that I can speak their language. We chatted a while about general, small topics, and then she explained that she had started a home-based care group that would visit the sick in the village and take medicine or food to them. She wondered if I could come and train them about HIV/AIDS and how it is transmitted. I quickly agreed and made arrangements to run a series of weekly workshops at the small village clinic.

Among the regular attendees at these sessions was a young woman in her 20s who sat quietly, listening intently. She was exceptionally thin for her height and walked with a slight limp. I noted her and wondered about her, but never approached her. During a special session, I invited a fellow Volunteer who was a retired nurse to make a presentation. When she was finished and final words were being spoken, the young woman stood up. She thanked me, and her smile and beautiful large eyes spoke volumes across cultures, across language barriers. Afterward, she asked if I could come and visit her. This was the beginning of a significant life lesson for me.

I went the following week to her home. She lived in a small, bare concrete house. Only one of the rooms had walls on all sides. Instead of inviting me in, we sat outside on two wire chairs, and she began to tell me her life story. She didn't know her father, and her mother had left her with her grandmother when she was a girl. She had three children, two of whom lived with relatives. I had often seen her third child in the village. Her current boyfriend, she told me, had given her AIDS. As she continued to talk, I inwardly despaired at the bleakness of her situation.

I was there to help, but nothing could prepare me for this woman's story. Nothing could prepare me for the hopelessness or helplessness I felt. She had no job, no money, and children to feed. There was

> *I was amazed that something so small as my simple hug could mean so much.*

no medication for her disease. She had full blown AIDS and would undoubtedly die within five years.

"Mabatu," she said, "I want to talk to people about my life. I want to warn other girls. You taught me so much. And you didn't just teach; you hugged me. No one ever hugs me because they are afraid they will catch AIDS. Thank you, Mabatu."

She wanted to share her story. I sat stunned, awed that she wanted to talk about her disease to people in a village where she could easily become ostracized. And I was amazed that something so small as my simple hug could mean so much.

I went to the local high schools and middle schools to ask if Angel could come and talk to the life skills classes. Though the teachers were hesitant, they knew a growing number of teenagers were dying of AIDS so they agreed that she could speak to the students.

By telling her story, Angel found confidence and a reason to live. She found a church and became part of a community. The challenges were still there, of course. Even my host mother would whisper and ask me why I bothered with such a woman. Yet, she realized, like so many others in my community, that Angel was worthy of being loved, she was worthy of *ubuntu*, which means treating fellow humans with dignity.

Toward the end of my service, Angel asked me to help her make a memory box for her daughters. As we sat together and prepared this box that would be given to her children after her death, I realized she was creating it not with sorrow, but with practicality and love.

I had started out the teacher, but in the end it was I who was taught. She taught me strength and survival and love. She taught me how to live.

I often complained about the small worries of life. Now, even so far away from Africa, I remember Angel, who learned to embrace her situation, prepare for it, and worked to help others along the way. She taught me that my problems are not so big that they cannot be conquered with courage. Angel still lives as far as I know, and I hope that the memories she has to give to her daughters—through the box she made and how she lived her life—will be many and unforgettable. Like Angel.

Barbara Arrington served as a Peace Corps Volunteer in South Africa from 2002 to 2004. She worked as a school and community resource Volunteer in a rural village in the province of Mpumalanga. One of her several community projects was working as an HIV/AIDS trainer to a home-based care group. She then worked as a volunteer coordinator with Habitat for Humanity.

¿Ya Ves? (Do You See It Now?)
Paul Ruesch · Mexico

I was 10 years old when I first visited Mexico. My family took a side trip to Tijuana after playing at Disneyland and along the beaches of San Diego. In addition to 10-cent comic books, I remember being fascinated by the strange color of the water and pungent odor that struck us while crossing a bridge over a large riverbed bordering the sprawling city. About 15 years later, I saw a newspaper photo of a river in South America with foam piled on it so high that cars were blocked from passing over a bridge. The caption stated that it was caused by an upstream factory, and that officials were "working to solve the problem." I wondered how, given that fairly simple, inexpensive technologies were readily available to prevent this type of contamination, this could still be happening anywhere in the world.

After 13 years working for the Environmental Protection Agency (EPA), and several trips abroad to conduct trainings and workshops in developing countries, I had come to realize that here in the U.S., we're very fortunate. We have a comprehensive set of environmental regulations to control air and water pollution discharges and ensure the proper management and disposal of wastes. In most developing countries, providing nourishment, education, employment, and basic infrastructure to support the population are the top priorities of the government. As a result, though it is recognized as being very important, minimum environmental controls exist. I asked myself—Was I ready to extend myself outside of my comfort zone in an attempt to make a difference in a foreign environment? Would my way of solving problems work in another culture? I decided that if I did not give it a try, I would never know—the moment had arrived to find out.

Peace Corps Mexico was born in 2004—with a special twist—the Mexican government specifically requested a small group of Volunteers with 10 to 15 years experience in business development, engineering or information technology to serve in its National Council for Science and Technology. The organization has research centers all over the country, which focus on providing assistance to targeted industries in a particular region, ranging from polymers to leather tanning to marine ecology. I arrived with the first group of just 14 Volunteers from among a wide range of ages, ethnicities, interests, and talents. I was surprised that, at age 36, I was actually one of the younger Volunteers, which consisted of many mid- to end-of-career, highly-trained, experienced, and motivated professionals.

Arriving at the home of my host family, Fer, one of the teenage sons, peered suspiciously over my shoulder as I announced I was a Peace Corps Volunteer. The only context in which he had heard the word "Corps" was related to the U.S. Marines and he asked if I was on a military mission and had a weapon. I would go on to answer the question "Why did you come here?" so many times over the next year, it was a good thing I had put some serious thought into my decision or I would have begun to wonder myself. Ironically, in a county where it seems everyone is a volunteer—with neighbors, in school, and at church—no one seemed to understand why an educated adult with a decent job and a home in the U.S. would leave everything to work for free away from his family. This was a country where, if you were able to achieve an education, you made the most of it and earned as much as you could in the highest position you could find. What I was doing there was a total mystery to those around me.

On the other hand, acceptance from the youngsters was rapid. They were quickly fascinated by the first *guero*, or light-skinned person, they had ever seen, along with the first spoken English they had ever heard. Everything I said, did, or carried with me fascinated the children in the neighborhood, and everyone would come running as I rounded the corner. The children didn't care who I was or why I had come, they were ready to play! Their capacity to stay outside, running around, was infinite and there seemed to be no curfew. I quickly realized I had met my match with this crew and was in for some of the most creative street games ever, none of which I ever won—which I was constantly reminded!

> *Everything I said, did, or carried with me fascinated the children in the neighborhood, and everyone would come running as I rounded the corner.*

At my assignment location, the Center for Innovative and Applied Technologies (CIATEC), my colleagues in the environmental group were startled by how little Spanish I spoke initially, but relieved at how similar much of the technical terminology is in both languages. Once at work, I quickly realized I was going to learn more than I could ever share with my coworkers, each holding master's or doctorate degrees in environmental engineering. Regardless, I soon learned that my field experience would prove invaluable in moving many of their advanced theories, experimental technologies, and laboratory techniques into commercial application in the field. I was immediately given a laptop and shown the full capacity of the center's environmental lab, complete with the latest analytical equipment that was capable of running a full range of chemical analyses.

When meeting with clients, I was frequently asked to speak directly with top level executives and engineers who were making decisions on various projects to make sure we were utilizing the best available and most economical environmental technology. In contrast to my host family, the most common questions I encountered here were: "How do they do this in the U.S.? How much will it cost? How fast can we get it done?" I was very fortunate to have many willing and able colleagues back home at EPA and in the environmental industry to help me find the right answers and share their expertise.

During my term, I was continuously amazed with the energy, drive, creativity, and ingenuity of the workers—they could fix or get anything up and running under seemingly impossible conditions with little or no tools, equipment, or materials. For one project, we were installing soil vent wells to bring oxygen and nutrients to micro-organisms feeding on subsurface contamination from a diesel fuel spill. My crew faced the seemingly impossible task of drilling the wells by hand among a maze of pipes carrying flammable liquids and gases with less than 12 inches of clearance between them. A field engineer named El Muñeco assured me by saying, *"Tranquilo, amigo, tranquilo"* (Calm down, my friend, calm down). He motioned with his hands to his crew, many of whom had spent their entire lives working within this maze of pipes, valves, and tanks. Once installed, for weeks everyone on the crew would say, *"Ya ves, guero?"* meaning "You see it now?" It was simply an affirmation that they could get any job done, any time, and without injuries.

The Peace Corps continues to rise to the challenge of recruiting a demographic of mid- and late-career professionals. Upon returning, I attended a seminar where the vice president of a large engineering firm stated, "Resumes of returned Peace Corps Volunteers always rise to the top of the pile (because we know we can) tell them to do everything, give them nothing, and know they'll get the job done." Without question, I now know that this is true—and that we learned it from the people we met and worked with during our service.

Returning to EPA, which had granted me the time off for my service, a whole new realm of opportunities awaited me. I am currently working on a project in which EPA is partnering with the U.S. Agency for International Development (USAID) to provide technical assistance to Central America in the area of solid waste management and recycling. With the knowledge I gained from my time in Mexico and fluency in Spanish, I am able to better work with Latin American countries in an official capacity and feel like I am truly making a difference. In fact, as I write this, I am preparing to address an audience of over 100 businesspeople on emerging environmental regulations and green technologies in Panama City. I can hear El Muñeco saying, "Tranquilo, amigo, tranquilo," and I'm sure I'll remember him saying to me afterwards, "ya ves?"

Paul served as an environmental engineer at the National Council of Science and Technology in Mexico from 2004 to 2006. He worked on several projects with Petroleros Mexicanos (PEMEX) in proper management of hazardous wastes and remediation of contaminated soils, ultimately establishing a team which continues to carry out similar projects within the national oil refinery system. After his service, Paul returned to his job at the United States EPA and is currently working on solid and hazardous waste projects throughout the Midwest and in Central America.

Talking of Trees

Aaron Welch · Dominican Republic

I had never cut down a tree before coming to the Dominican Republic as a Peace Corps Volunteer. Fresh out of training, I understood my job to be simple: I was going to plant trees. Then why did I find myself, in my first weeks in the village, hacking away at sturdy Caribbean pines on the slopes above the village where I was to spend the next two years?

When I spoke of deforestation, villagers told me, "We have trees," and they would point to the ridge tops. They were right; many pine trees did grow on the hills and ridges around the village, clumped here and there between fallow fields of waist-high grass and steep, brown slopes of plowed earth opened up for beans and other cash crops.

"But trees are life," I would protest. This was the slogan of an ubiquitous nonprofit in the region, and a phrase I could easily repeat in Spanish.

"Yes, it's very important," the villagers would agree with me.

Months later I would come to understand the Dominican, "It's very important," meant the same as a slowly muttered "uh-huh" at home. I became frustrated when I heard it, and recognized that it signaled reaching a dead end.

But I didn't know this at the beginning, so I hiked into the hills with a group of men from the village and cut down pine trees that had been damaged in a hurricane two years earlier. The damage wasn't

> *I learned to linger in the village stores, or* colmaldos, *where women buy the rice and beans for the day's lunch and other supplies.*

always obvious, and I felt uneasy about felling trees, especially considering I had been sent to the village to plant more. But I consoled myself with the knowledge that the outing at least provided an opportunity to talk about trees.

In fact, I took every opportunity I could to talk of trees in those early days; of how the hurricane had done away with nearly all the large, old trees along the river; the necessity of trees to the hydrologic cycle; the benefits of trees on the farm, for soil conservation, shade, and as wind breaks. And always I was told, "It's very important." But never in those first months did I manage to inspire any of the villagers to work with me to plant any. Gradually, I spoke less of trees. I became bored with my well-rehearsed entreaties. My Spanish improved, and I found, much to everyone's enjoyment, that I could talk of other things. I began to attend to the daily business of living in a Dominican village.

I made regular visits to the many colorfully painted homes scattered up and down the narrow valley. Mostly, this meant sipping strong coffee, freshly brewed the moment a visitor was seen coming up the path. Sometimes there was much conversation; other times I simply sat and enjoyed the cool breeze blowing through the mountain village. Always, my hosts served the coffee in a tiny cup atop a saucer. To be given a saucer was a sign of respect in a village where there are not enough saucers to go around. I appreciated the gesture and made sure I held onto the saucer, keeping my cup on it between sips.

I learned to linger in the village stores, or *colmaldos*, where women buy the rice and beans for the day's lunch, and other supplies. Occasionally, I would share a Fanta with someone in the colmaldo that day—there were always two or three people passing time at the counter or on the bench under the shade outside. Two stores became my regular hangouts, and visiting them helped shape what became my daily routine. My visits came to be expected, and I enjoyed my newfound place in the community.

Each day, when I returned from my visits, I entertained a gaggle of *muchachos* (boys) on the tiny cement porch at the front of my faded pink house. I was popular for the tin can of crayons and sheets of scrap paper I kept inside. We bathed in the river on hot afternoons and played games on the patch of dry earth behind my house. If I needed a packet of coffee or an egg to go with lunch, I could always send one of the children to the colmaldo with a peso or two, enough to get whatever I needed and a hard candy for the muchacho.

One afternoon, at a meeting of the village women's group, the topic of trees came up. I had been helping the women to expand a vegetable garden, and we were discussing new seeds they might plant. I heard a voice in the room say something about fruit trees, and I remembered the original reason I came here. I promised the women we would have fruit trees. I didn't know how we would make this happen, but a renewed sense of purpose rushed over me, and I decided to worry about the details later.

The details proved to be many, and my second year in the village was consumed by attending to each one. The women and I had resolved to create a tree nursery in the village; a site had to be selected, a fence erected, weeds cleared, and tools and materials had to be found. Most difficult of all, we needed support from the rest of the village. But, unlike my first months, now I wasn't the only one talking about trees. This time there were 24 women speaking about trees louder—and more fluently— than me.

The women organized workdays in the tree nursery. As the project grew, I found myself working nearly every day on the parcel of land we had selected. Then the women began to schedule staggered workdays so that at least one or two of them would be there to help me. They used their considerable leverage to get the men in the village to help build the nursery and a neighboring shed to house the tools and shelter the truck-load of dark topsoil the government had donated. Slowly, a tree nursery started to take shape.

Now, when I made visits to my friends' colorful homes, or shared a Fanta at the colmaldo, people were talking to me about trees. Even the muchachos were excited. They used my tin can of crayons to draw me pictures of trees we were growing. I shared their excitement, and when the nursery was fully functional, I decided it was time to hang the large sign I had secretly made. The sign named the nursery after the women's group. The women gathered, and we admired the results of our work.

"We have trees," the women declared.

They were right. The tree nursery was half filled with saplings organized neatly into rows of black plastic bags full of dark soil. The sandy germination beds were planted with seeds of a dozen different species. Trees would be planted in the village in a few months' time. Together, we had created something that had the potential to grow and benefit the entire community and the land the community depends upon.

"It's very important," I said with a smile.

Aaron Welch served as an agroforestry Volunteer in the Dominican Republic from 2000 to 2002. He holds a master's degree in environmental science from Yale University, where he was the recipient of the School of Forestry and Environmental Studies' Returned Peace Corps Volunteer scholarship.

The Faces of an Acacia Tree

Karin Vermilye • *Cameroon*

The Cameroonian sky was threatening as the dark rumbling clouds shifted their way quickly toward us, and the kids finished patting down the earth around the last tree. Together, that day in June 2002, we planted 30 trees. It was a small amount in the face of so much sand and nutrient-hungry soil, but a step. A slight breeze was blowing that soothed the prickle of salt on my sweaty skin. Little pieces of paper, with their French and mathematical equations, fluttered past in the savanna grass. I remember squatting next to the last tree we had planted, watching as the students and the teachers gathered up the hoes and shovels. I remember feeling the tiny, delicate, light green leaves with my fingers, and I remember how I saw so many people's efforts within that skinny, young acacia tree.

The Seeds

Alphonse gave us the acacia seeds in November. We had been working with him to develop his small tree nursery into a commercial tree business. We helped him to formulate a business plan by scratching figures into the sand in his yard with a small stick. We were calculating how much money he could make if he grew and sold such and such amount of trees for this and that amount of money. That day in November, we told him about the tree nursery at the school.

"Wait," he exclaimed and ran into his hut. He came out with an

> *Over pounded millet and greenleaf sauces, perhaps with a side of bony fish, we would discuss our days.*

old, yellow, rusted, powdered milk can. He took the plastic lid slowly off the top and told me to hold out my hands. I watched as he poured the slick, brown, shiny seeds from the metal can into my cupped palms. They were small seeds; three could fit on my thumbnail. "These will help," he said. "They are from a strong tree." I wrapped the seeds into a corner of my red bandanna, and put them deep into my pocket.

The Soil

My friend Hapsatou told us where the good soil might be. "Behind the old school," she said. "I have heard it is good there." *"La bonne terre,"* Hapsatou had said. The good earth. Ah, my friend Hapsatou. Almost every night for the two years we lived in Touroua, we ate dinner with her and her family. Over pounded millet and greenleaf sauces, perhaps with a side of bony fish, we would discuss our days. As my French improved, I worked at describing all the details of what had happened that day. We would tell her who we had seen, what they had said, and how all the trees in the nurseries scattered around the village were growing. She was so eager for contact and for information.

Hapsatou was a married Muslim woman in a very traditional area. Our village in the north of Cameroon practiced wife seclusion. This means that once a woman is married, she does not often leave her home. There are some exceptions. She can venture from her compound walls if one of her children is sick so she can go to the clinic or the marabou. She can also leave to attend a wedding or a funeral or if one of her friends is sick or giving birth. With this practice, the children become the women's messengers, running from house to house exchanging the news and gossip.

In the first few months I was there, my stomach often revolted against the new foods and the heat that were so foreign to me. Hapsatou's five-year-old son El Kass would come to visit us and see me lying in the hammock or outside the doorway on a mat.

"*Jabamma, El Kass,*" I would say. Welcome.

"*Jam na, Kareen?*" he would ask me in the traditional Fulfulde greeting that meant literally, "Do you have peace?"

"*Jam ne, El Kass.*" It's all good.

"*Jam bandu na?*" How's your body?

"*Na boddum, sobajo am.*" Not good, my friend.

At this, El Kass would turn and run home, without even bothering to finish the traditional string of greetings, including how's the work, how's your house, how are your goats, how are the fields, and how's the heat (which would always make him giggle). He would tell Hapsatou that I was, once again, *mal au ventre.*

This made me a source of freedom for her. She would come over as soon as she heard I wasn't feeling well, bringing with her a bowl of thick and sweetened *bouille.* The thick, milky porridge was usually slightly flavored with lemons and was a wonderful combination of sweet and sour. I would lie on the mat sipping the bouille while she sat next to me. She would talk about the plants she thought I should know, and tell me who was good to work with in the village and whom to avoid.

The first time we walked through our village together was on the way to my first funeral. Hapsatou, her husband Abba, my husband Brian, and I had walked into the compound together when we first arrived. Hapsatou motioned me one way as I watched Brian and Abba disappear behind one of the red mud walls.

Then I heard the crying. I peeked inside the hut and saw 35 women, packed shoulder-to-shoulder within the dark interior. Many of the women were steadily and quietly crying while rocking forward and back. Then, one old woman with wrinkled hands reached out to me in greeting, entwined her fingers within mine, opened her mouth, and let out a long and loud wail. The feeling was surreal, surrounded by weeping women in a wailing hut in Cameroon, but Hapsatou's eyes caught mine, and she steadied me.

> *So many hands were involved in giving life to that acacia tree.*

My friend Hapsatou, who had wrapped me so well in her nourishment, had given us directions to the most productive soil in town, even though she could not walk there herself.

The Water

Abduli was dressed in his long, pale brown robe that reached to his knees, with the matching pants below. The sweat was beading on his forehead and rolling down onto his lips. He blew the droplets off his pursed lips, and concentrated on flipping the black rubber bucket just right so it would fill quickly. When he was satisfied and felt the tug of the right weight of water on the rope, he pulled the bucket hand-over-hand, back to the surface. He poured the water into the silver metal bucket sitting in a puddle by the well. He did this several times until the water lapped at the rim of the metal bucket.

Then, he carefully started to lift the bucket to his head. His friend Amadou spotted him and came to help lift the heavy load. Together, they placed the sloshing container on Abduli's head and spilled but a few drops. Abduli slowly walked to the corner of the yard where the tree nursery was and filled the watering cans. The watering cans were old plastic containers with holes punched in the top, but they worked acceptably. He made two more trips to the well and back to make sure all the seedlings were watered. Then he washed his hands and head and finally took a long drink from the well.

So many hands were involved in giving life to that acacia tree. It came to exist through the effort of the community, and the interest of individuals. In a few years, that tree will become tall and thorny, with a dense flat crown and dark fissured bark. Each of its branches will tell the story of the man who gathered the seeds, the woman who knew where the good soil was, the students who pulled the water from the well, and all the others who worked to plant green trees on the dusty land.

Karin Vermilye worked as a forestry extension agent while a Peace Corps Volunteer. She and her husband, Brian App, served in Cameroon in the Sahel Agroforestry Program from 2000 to 2002. Karin was a participant in Peace Corps' Master's International program through the University of Montana, and earned a master's in resource conservation in May 2004.

Women Can Learn Things, Too

Amber B. Davis-Collins • Honduras

C erro Grande was a two-hour walk up the mountain from my town of San Pedro de Tutule. The dirt road ended abruptly about a mile before arrival—a government project gone awry. Instead, patrons of this little community at the top of the mountain (population 110) had two choices—a steep, slick trail that took about 20 minutes from the dirt road, or a more gentle approach that took twice as long. I always chose the latter, which ended near Don José and Doña Maria's house.

I originally met Don José at a baby weighing in Granadillo. This is a community event where mothers bring their children to be weighed so that adequate nutrition and healthy development can be tracked. I was about three-fourths of the way through my Peace Corps service at the time. He had heard that the *gringa* in Tutule had vegetable seeds and wanted some for his family. He was the only man in attendance at the baby weighing that day. In fact, Don José was the only man I ever saw at a baby weighing during my two years in Honduras. He didn't speak until every child had been weighed and most of the women had taken their children and returned home.

"They tell me that you have seeds," he said, not looking at my face.

"Yes," I answered. "But today I have only carrots." I handed him a packet.

"Do you want me to come to your house and help when you plant?"

I asked, hoping that I hadn't offended him.

"Yes, please," he whispered. "I live in Cerro Grande," he said, pointing to the top of the mountain. And so our friendship began.

On my first visit two days later, none of his six children spoke to me. Five of them stood behind their mother, Doña Maria, while Don José made introductions. The other, still too young to walk, stayed in Doña Maria's arms and wailed. Doña Maria appeared sullen and withdrawn. The two-room house was made of rocks, sticks, and mud. A ragged dog tended to its scraggly pup next to the earthen stove.

The kids giggled and ducked their faces when I directed my small talk toward them, but none mustered up the courage to reply. "They have never seen a white person before," said Doña Maria flatly, as if this explained everything. And I guess it did. In an area of the world that still didn't have electricity, much less radios or televisions, my blond hair, blue eyes, and pale skin must have been quite a spectacle.

All the children except the youngest came out to watch Don José and me plant the garden that afternoon. A few of the neighbors came, too. We were obviously the biggest entertainment venue in town that day. As we worked, I asked about the school that I had passed on my way up the mountain. "The teacher almost never comes," Don José explained. "It's been too rainy and the walk is just too long."

"That's terrible!" I exclaimed.

Don José shrugged his shoulders. "The boys aren't old enough for school yet."

I looked over at the two oldest children, both girls, standing shyly at the edge of the garden. "What about the girls?" I asked.

Don José laughed. "They have work to do."

As I pressed on, Don José revealed that his wife had never gone to school and that he himself had only gone for two years. That's all that he was going to require of his sons, too, provided that the school ever got a regular teacher. "But there's no one in Cerro Grande that can teach," he added softly.

Over the next few months, I trekked up the mountain every week or so to check on the garden, as well as to visit Don José and his family. More often than not, Don José was away, and I would end up passing the time with Doña Maria and the children instead. I brought more seeds—onions, sweet peppers,

> *As time went by, this woman who I once dreaded visiting because she seemed so bitter, began to open up.*

and radishes. We talked a lot about gardening—the importance of thinning and weeding, how often to water, and how a diversified diet would make her family healthier (their nutritional regime at the time consisted of corn, beans, and an occasional bit of rice). She and the children worked in the garden with me when I visited, but most of the work was done when I wasn't around. It wasn't long before shoots started springing up.

As time went by, this woman who I once dreaded visiting because she seemed so bitter, began to open up. We talked about her family and her life before she married José. Doña Maria's past had not been rich with opportunity. Although she never said it, and probably didn't even realize it, I could tell that a difficult life had left her emotionally numb. But things were changing—she began to smile and talk excitedly each time I arrived at the house. She greeted me with an ear of corn and laughed when I played with the kids. There was a definite transformation in the house of Don José and Doña Maria.

On one of my last trips up the mountain before I completed my service, Don José was home. I began my visit with the obligatory soccer match with the children. (The ball was an ancient wadded plastic bag tied into a ball shape with a piece of string.) Afterwards, the entire family moved out to the garden to admire the work that everyone had done over the last few months.

Standing in the garden, Don José pulled a mature carrot out of the ground. "You know," he said thoughtfully. "I'm really glad that you have been helping Maria. Because of you, I have realized that women can learn things, too."

My first reaction as an educated woman was to laugh because I was sure that he was joking. But when I looked at his face, I saw that he was serious. And the stark realization for me was that this was a totally new insight for Don José. After I was able to close my gaping jaw, I met his smile with one of my own. In the background I could hear Doña Maria laughing.

Amber B. Davis-Collins served as a crop extensionist Volunteer in Honduras from 2002 to 2004. She has a master's degree in agricultural education from the University of Georgia. Amber worked in the pesticides program of the U.S. Environmental Protection Agency in Atlanta and was awarded a bronze medal by the agency for her work with Latino farm worker issues.

The Work Continues
Kelly Daniel · Kenya

Her name is Irene and her breath comes in ragged blasts, like the sound of an old bicycle pump pushing air as best it can. Her family waits for that sound to fall silent. It will not be long.

The day before I stand in Irene's house, so deep into the bush that the women I'm with point out crushed branches and limbs, saying, "Elephant," I stand in front of bored high school students, kept a day beyond school's closing by a paperwork snafu. I run through my bag of tricks, barren, after only 10 weeks of trying to teach HIV/AIDS prevention, close the session, and field questions from a few students interested or scared enough to stay behind. A sharp-eyed teen named Diana looks me over. "These people who have AIDS, what do you do for them?" she asks. Words tumble from my mouth, a jumble of platitudes. Diana cuts into my ramble. "But what do you *do* for them?" "I try," I answer at last.

Irene lies on a double bed that allows no other furniture into the room that holds her, her mother, eight of my companions, and me. I am with an AIDS group newly trained in home-based care for patients across our 10 villages. This is our first visit. All I know of our patient before we arrive is that she is terribly sick. She is more than that. The jovial mood of the eight good friends on the hike to this tiny house has vanished; grim, but not horrified expressions are on every face. I look around the *manyatta*—the circular huts of mud-stick-grass splayed across so much of

> *Luckily, there is a single moment when I do know what needs to be done, having somehow picked up knowledge over the years of the proper way to turn a bedridden patient.*

Africa—and listen to the rasps coming from the bed. Diana's question swims in my head.

Irene is caught in a state of "not." Not really living; not quite dead. She no longer moves, sees, hears. She feels pain, heard in the wretched whimpers echoing from the bed when two of our group bathe her. I know almost nothing about her, save her name, what is killing her, and where she will die. I do not know her age, but guess that she is no more than in her early 30s. My age.

Her father sits outside with a younger man (perhaps her husband?) and three children, at least one of whom is hers. I do know that she is loved. Her mother, her own long life evidenced by a leathery face and wisps of grey hair visible beneath her head wrap, moves from the head of the bed to the foot, to the door frame and back, never out of sight. She does not speak to her daughter while we are there, but her hands are always reaching out. Her fingers peck at the blankets, rearranging them constantly. Her hands know they do not have much longer to touch this life they held first, and most often. I sit and watch.

The group believes I know more than they do about providing care for AIDS patients. I do not, and have not been able to get them to understand this. They will turn to me for guidance and reassurance throughout the day.

Luckily, there is a single moment when I do know what needs to be done, having somehow picked up knowledge over the years of the proper way to turn a bedridden patient. I stand at the footboard as Alice, tall and regal, feeds Irene *uji*, a porridge/millet mixture. Lydia, squat, plump, and funny, is at Alice's elbow, swatting blasted flies that are taking advantage of the fact that Irene's eyes are perpetually half opened, her mouth in the same repose. The mother stands at the headboard, fingers cupping Irene's small head, raising it slightly for the waiting spoon. A sound like a blocked drain unclogging is the only cue that Irene has swallowed the food, and Alice delivers another spoonful. Lydia has the look of someone who wishes she had something more substantial to do. I know that look. I stand and watch these four women and am filled with such a sense of love, of blessing, that I nearly explode into tears. Later, the anger will come: how unnecessary, this disease, these losses! The slender, gentle sets of fingers gripping the spoon, the head, the blanket, the air where a fly was; those are what affect me and what I remember.

Most of my time these last few weeks has been spent at the opposite end of the spectrum, with school children, most of whom do not have HIV/AIDS. And we want to keep it that way. I've taught 11 basic HIV lessons in seven schools so far. I'm quicker on my feet than I've any right to be—given the shortness of time in this role—in fielding questions from kids, many of whom want nothing more than to embarrass the *mzungu* who has come to talk to them about sex, death, life, and disease. It's impossible to be self-conscious in these moments, so absurd are the scenarios, so surreal the situations.

AIDS in Kiswahili, by the way, is *Ukimwi*. I've yet to find someone who can translate "HIV." So many Kiswahili words are borrowed from the Arab, Portuguese, and English conquerors of East Africa in millennia past that some phrases have no alternate and the Kiswahili speaker just stands, blinking, when I ask how to say something like avocado in the language. "Avocado," he or she answers. Oh.

My eight companions and I ride back to Ndome, having hiked more kilometers than I know that morning. The women sing the buoyant, joyous songs all Kenyan women sing en route somewhere, even if it is just from the kitchen to the sitting room. Our packed little posse bounces along the dirt, a parade of song, as the driver turns up the road to my dispensary. I sit there, remembering in that moment the rise and fall of the green blanket across Irene's miserable chest, and I look at the smiling faces of the women I am with and their happiness at a long walk deferred. Extreme highs, extreme lows, dozens of them packed into each day. Always, among the saddest moments, a reminder of the joys that fill this world. I feel blessed for the ability to take it all in.

Irene died the next day. The work continues.

Kelly Daniel served as a public health Volunteer in Kenya from 2003 to 2005. She joined the Peace Corps after a career in newspaper journalism.

Cultural *Understanding*

"Lessons from our region show that peace must be built between peoples. It derives from understanding, trust, and a sense of working toward a shared destiny. It arises only out of mutual and equitable exchange of skills, of ideas, of cultural values. Peace Corps Volunteers—going where they are invited; bringing open minds, dedication, and enthusiasm; living and working side by side with their hosts; and returning with new perspectives to share with those at home—are among the best examples of how that peace will be achieved."

Queen Noor Al Hussein, Jordan

Going the Distance
Curtis Blyden · Mongolia

A public relations announcement for the Peace Corps asks, "Life is calling. How far will you go?"

Traveling from Boston, Massachusetts, to Bulgan, Mongolia, may have indicated that I was willing to go pretty far, but I soon learned about the underlying message within that question. It is more than a matter of physical distance, it's a testament to how far one is willing to stretch his or her emotions.

After the first of two years in Mongolia, I realized I was willing to go pretty far in that department as well. After all, I went from being Michael Jordan, to becoming Harry Potter, to being addressed simply as "brother!" Can anyone top that?

Before explaining, I should note that I don't have a life inspiring story about why I joined the Peace Corps, but my life was inspired because of the choice I made. My decision to join was mainly based on the fact I wanted to live overseas, and encourage development within a developing country. I had always known about the Peace Corps and suppose the idea of joining had been in the back of my mind, but I was out of college for about a year before I actually made the leap. Prior to my Mongolia experience, my overseas experience was limited to a semester in London. Mongolia and London are definitely two worlds apart, but I knew I wanted to experience another culture and the Peace Corps just seemed like a logical step.

> *I soon discovered that you can learn a lot from children. They don't really care if you're fluent in their language, they just want you to spend time with them.*

Which brings me to how I went from being called the world's most famous basketball player, to a fictional character from a chronology of books sold all over the globe, to simply being considered a member of the family. As a black man, I don't fit the stereotype many people have of Americans. In Mongolia, they typically picture America as "white." However, Michael Jordan is black and people realize he is from America, so that moniker was affixed to me after I made the mistake of trying to dunk a basketball at a community event. The dunk wasn't very successful, but being a 6-foot-2 black man with a bald head, I was soon being addressed as Michael Jordan. However, it wasn't long before I was transformed into Harry Potter. I don't really know the reason for this. Maybe it's just easy for Mongolian children to pronounce. I would laugh about it and joke with the kids.

As a youth development Volunteer, I got to know a lot of them in Bulgan, the village where I was based. There, over 3,000 children live among a population of approximately 16,000, and I soon discovered that you can learn a lot from children. They don't really care if you're fluent in their language, they just want you to spend time with them. There were times when we would be playing and having the greatest time in the world, and I wouldn't know a word they were saying.

My work as a Volunteer was to provide children with life skills training and recreational opportunities; teach English and computer skills; and lead forums on such topics as sexually transmitted diseases and human trafficking. A local project that was among my proudest moments was an NCAA-style basketball tournament we held, with over 100 kids participating. I was able to secure jerseys from the Boston Celtics and distributed them. The Celtics are probably the most popular team in Mongolia as a result.

Boston and Bulgan have the same number of syllables in their names, but that's where the similarities end. Landlocked by Russia to the north and China to the south, Mongolia is difficult to get to, but

> *There were certainly days in Mongolia when I was ready to go home, but I now know I would do it again in a minute.*

once you are there you will find some of the most beautiful people you'll ever meet. I was really pampered my first year there because everyone wanted to be my host, not just in the country, but in their community and in their homes. Of course, I ran into my fair share of culture shock. A poor village, Bulgan is much like the Old West. It wasn't uncommon to see men racing their horses down the street. It also took some time to adjust to the food. I remember when my host father pulled me out of my room to help with the cooking. One moment the family was bringing a sheep through the house and the next there was a slaughterhouse in my kitchen. They threw the head in the refrigerator and for two weeks after that I attempted to become a vegetarian. Drinking horse milk, another local custom, also required me to work up some courage, but after awhile I really got to like it. When I first started, my family would be rolling and laughing because they hadn't seen many Americans willing to drink horse milk. By the time I had ended my homestay, I was drinking it with the best of them!

So did my time in Peace Corps Mongolia change me? I would say it did in subtle ways. One of the most important things I learned is that the world has so much to offer when we think outside of the box. After experiencing America from the inside, as well as the outside, I've found there is so much to be gained from meeting those from other countries. Doing so has left me feeling more optimistic about the future. I have learned we are all bound by two basic goals: we all want to live in relative peace and harmony with our neighbors; and everyone wants to be respected, not only for their views, but for their culture and way of life.

There were certainly days in Mongolia when I was ready to go home, but I now know I would do it again in a minute. The turning point was when I was taken out of the context of just being a Peace Corps Volunteer living in Mongolia. The point where someone would see me on the street and simply address me as "brother." I knew I had become a member of the family.

Curtis Blyden served as a youth development Volunteer in Mongolia from 2005 to 2007. He joined the Peace Corps one year after getting his degree in political science and criminal justice from Curry College in Milton, Massachusetts, just outside of Boston. He currently works for City Year in Boston, a nonprofit organization that provides mentoring and other services to underserved children and youth.

Hope Dies Last
Patrick Burns • *Moldova*

I travel because I like to explore, I explore because I like to learn, I learn because I like to understand. It was with these thoughts in mind that I set out for Peace Corps/Moldova in June 2003. Since then, it has been one lesson after the next.

When I landed in my pre-service training village of Mereseni, it was very quiet, hot, and dusty. I remember thinking to myself that this is where I'll spend the next 10 weeks of my life learning the Romanian language, Moldovan culture, and a lot about myself. My host family was warm, friendly, and very hospitable. This meant they would offer me their best *vin de casa* (wine of the house) upon my entering through the gate. Immediately, I realized this was unlike any other wine I'd ever tasted. It was very young and tasted more like fortified grape juice than the wine I was used to drinking in other countries. However, I accepted their generosity and drank a glass. I was able to have a conversation at about a two-year-old level, which was a very humbling experience and reminded me of when I was an exchange student in Mexico during the early 1980s. I knew that the language would come, just how fast and at what speed remained to be seen. Two days later, I had my answer: six hours a day of language training at an amazing pace. What a way to go—and it works!

My fondest memory of the village is a little seven-year-old girl named Irina. She had a beautiful smile and a curiosity as to what the American was doing in her village. Moreover, she had the patience to practice Romanian with me, a 41-year-old Volunteer. As the summer went on, I started teaching her English words and she'd sit outside the gate and wait for me to get home from school. She always wanted to know what I had learned that day. One day I received a care package from my mother back home and it contained Oreos. I gave Irina a sleeve and she sat there with the biggest smile you could imagine and ate them all. After a while the group got larger, and I was up to seven in this informal learning group. They learned from me, and I learned from them. I learned that, at times, the Peace Corps makes corporate America seem slow; we accomplish more in an hour than some firms do in a week. There are times when we move at lightspeed, times when the clock seems to stand still, and times when it appears to run in reverse.

During pre-service training, I was assigned to teach business English at a local university in the capital of Chisinau. At the end of my three-week course, one of my students came up to me and gave me a kiss on the cheek because she was so excited to practice and improve her English. This was very special because she's an English teacher here in Moldova. Another student brought me a gift from her village. My students were so passionate to learn that it was difficult to understand how Moldova could be so poor. But the next generation has hope. In Moldova, there is a saying, *"Speranta moare ultima!"* (Hope dies last!)

There were times when I'd wonder what sort of an impact the Peace Corps and I were having on Moldova and my students. The best answers I can give are the following examples. First, my wife, Rosie, and I wanted to travel back home to see our ill fathers as they were both coping with diseases. Upon telling my students that we'd be going to Seattle, two of them asked if they could see us off at the train station. "Of course," I responded. When we met Vadim and Cristina at the train station, they were holding two boxes of local chocolates and two bottles of Moldovan wine.

Cristina said, "These are for your parents. We want to thank them for having you!" I know that those chocolates never tasted better or the wine smoother.

The second example happened during one of my English language club meetings before the Christmas holiday during my first year as a Volunteer. I asked the group to write an answer to the question, "If there was a Santa Claus, what would you want him to bring Moldova?"

One of the students in the group responded, "Freedom, and the knowledge to know how to use it." This remarkable answer led to a discussion of what it means to be free, the rights and responsibilities that we share when we live in a democracy, and the importance of improving ourselves to better our future and our community's future.

I believe that the most important thing we do as Volunteers is provide hope. Everything else seems like an ancillary detail. This sounds so easy doesn't it? That's because we're Americans, and we were born with a sense of optimism that doesn't always exist elsewhere. A British friend once told me that he thinks Americans have an optimism chip planted in our heads at birth. And so it goes.

To my friends, colleagues, and students in Moldova who helped me understand, *"Multumesc mult!"* (Thank you very much!)

"Speranta moare ultima!"

Patrick Burns served as a Volunteer in Moldova from 2003 to 2005. He joined the Peace Corps after 18 years as a stockbroker/sales manager. Following his service, he began pursuing a career at the U.S. Department of State as a foreign service officer.

Soybean Transformations
John Sheffy • Togo

I arrived in Togo in June 2002 with 20 other Peace Corps trainees. Some of us, like me, were assigned to work in the area of natural resource management and agriculture, and others would be small business development Volunteers. The Peace Corps took the small business Volunteers to their training site, Kpalime, the main regional market city and a paradise of Togolese movers and shakers. Our training group went directly to live with our host families and received an immersion into Togo village life. Suddenly we had no electricity and the only running water was the water your host sister carried from the river and you poured from a cup over your head. Over the next 11 weeks, we attended information sessions on everything from feeding chickens to feeding ourselves; vegetable gardening to garnering understanding of HIV/AIDS; mapping village resources to managing local customs.

After training, I was assigned to Kuma-Dunyo, a highland village of 300 farmers. It was early September, the end of the rainy season, when I arrived. The village awoke before dawn. When I arose at 7 a.m., all the compounds were empty, *foyers* (mud stoves) left smoking; it was almost like the villagers had abandoned their camp and moved on. Everyone had already gone to farm during the few good hours of the lifting fog before the sky darkened and the rains began. Armed with my French *dictionnaire de poche* (pocket dictionary), I followed, leaping over rivers of ants on their perpetual search for somewhere higher to hide from getting washed away.

Once at the fields, it became apparent right away that I knew nothing about traditional agriculture. I hand gestured and grunted my way into the ranks of farmers, plunging countless node-covered, red-colored sticks into ridges of red-colored earth. The old man cutting up the branches for us to plant corrected me as I went. My nodes were usually pointed in the wrong direction and the angle at which I stuck my sticks was too steep. In front of my gang of planters were the diggers, overturning the rich top layer of soil by hand with crooked, arm-length hoes. They worked in what seemed like the most awkward body position possible, bent over, shoveling between their legs, like swinging a maul while playing Twister. This was all part of the manioc-growing ritual, a means of starch production that sustained the village.

These field visits went on for weeks, every day a revelation of crops, trail systems, and work songs; women, the foundation of all village life, balancing loads of leaves, tubers, and firewood on their heads. They were doing the hardest work with the most stamina I have seen. But, unless measured by blisters and insect bites, my daily tromps didn't seem to be getting me any closer to being an effective Volunteer. Over fogged-in morning silence and the numbing static of evening rain on my aluminum roof, I dreamt of integrated conservation and development projects. I fantasized about calling meetings with the elders, defining the village's needs, facilitating brainstorming sessions, and drawing multicolored flipcharts to match the color of fields. I fantasized about flipcharts; I needed something to do.

My house was in the southwest corner of the village, by the *moulin* (mill) and avocado forest, in one of the village's five clans. I heard stories that elders of each clan and the chief make up a village development committee. I visited the committee members several times a week, asking them when their next meeting would be. The response was always the same: "This week we'll be meeting for sure." But the meetings never came, and gradually I stopped going to the fields. It was November and the dry season's harmattan winds had thrown sand in the sky. During communal labor one morning, when the debris was swept off the public sitting space into the road and burned, the haze blew in a smoky screen. In a few days, the haze seemed like it was always there and would never go away.

At this time, I was grasping the languages and studying the six-inch stack of handouts we were given during training. It took a month to wade through the case studies from past Volunteer projects. It was like someone had run through a library and torn a page out of every book; yet, over time, I organized the papers into chapters. That's how badly I needed to organize something. One chapter was on food preservation and transformation techniques.

Men had pulled my leg enough times with the old "village development meeting" joke while their wives sweated over the cooking fire that I decided this chapter could be of use. I swept the village; hit all 62 kitchens, telling everyone to meet in the sitting place on *Mercredi* (Wednesday) to learn how to use *soja* (soy). On Tuesday, I rode my bike to town, 30 minutes screaming down the mountains, three hours slugging back up. We didn't have soy in our village market, so I bought the equivalent of $2 worth of dried soybeans, which was a backpack full.

After soaking the beans overnight, I gathered my cooking gear and began making trips to the meeting place to get ready. On my first trip, a few ladies were sitting on the half log benches socializing. They were wrapped in colorful, mismatching *pagne* (printed cloth) costumes like they were going to church or the market. It was obvious something was astir. By the time we started heating the first giant *marmite* (pot) of water, at least 40 women were present. Although I hadn't invited them, there were at least as many men there, too, standing in a circle outside the women as if supervising, but not there to learn. Were villagers that interested in free food?

I quickly recognized that soy had little to do with this meeting. This was about me, my fantasy village meeting, and wild potential scenarios. How would I get everyone to participate? What would the village priorities be? Would there be an elaborate decision-making ceremony

> *They all seemed to be asking the same question I was asking myself: What is this American doing here? And my response was... soybeans?*

between the elders? Was I ready? I had spent the last three days reading all my notes about soy, wondering if using my blue cloth as a filter would make blueberry soy milk, and why in the world I was giving open-fire cooking lessons to village mamas who could reach their bare hands into a boiling pot of water with a smile. I scanned the crowd of eyes looking back at me. They all seemed to be asking the same question I was asking myself: What is this American doing here? And my response was... soybeans?

As I scribbled my first flipchart notes and the cooking fire battled the smoky, harmattan winds to keep the soy boiling, I began to feel like I was drawing a treasure map for a crew of pirates. But the pirates knew the map all along. The village had not been waiting for me; not looking for someone to organize village meetings or facilitate its development. The people didn't need me to figure out what was wrong.

I was answering Ama's questions about my age and why I wasn't married. I was questioning Madame Comfort's cooking critique, that one must never change their stirring direction. I was trying to explain to Yawa why more sugar doesn't always taste better. At the same time, I was doling out samples of soy couscous to bashful members of the crowd and spouting the values of soy from nutritional, environmental, and economic standpoints. Somehow the people were listening, asking questions, and having a great time.

My role seemed to solidify as the soy milk curdled into cheese. I wasn't starring in the film, *Bringing Soy to the Village*; I was part of an experiment. There wasn't going to be a Volunteer project like digging a well or building a school. As time went by, I learned what was important to people and where they wanted me to intervene. I formed friendships with them that allowed us to discuss realities of problems, not myths about what I should be doing and what they should be wanting. That day, we filtered our soy and ourselves out of the smokescreen and ate our efforts—efforts we tasted over the next two years of experimenting with assumptions and learning as things constantly changed, leaving an aftertaste that lingers on my tongue to this day.

John Sheffy served as a natural resource management Volunteer in Togo from 2002 to 2004. As a Master's International participant, he conducted the field research for his thesis on participatory forest management in the Ghana-Togo highlands while serving in the Peace Corps.

Saying Goodbye
Caroline Chambre · Burkina Faso

It hardly seems possible that two years ago I was watching, more than a little teary-eyed, as the official Peace Corps Land Cruiser pulled away from my new home and headed slowly out of my village. I had heard stories of Volunteers being dropped off in their new homes, only to go quickly chasing after the vehicle exclaiming, "Wait— I'm not ready yet!" I had laughed at those stories at the time, but as the Land Cruiser faded from sight, I felt a kinship with those fabled Volunteers, understanding now how it felt to realize you were on your own in a place that seemed so foreign to anything you had ever known. With a combination of euphoria and trepidation, I waved one last goodbye at the car that couldn't even be seen anymore, turned, and walked slowly toward my house to start my life as a Peace Corps Volunteer in Mahon, Burkina Faso.

It's now two years later and last week I was the one driving away, being waved at by a crowd of villagers as I officially ended my service and said goodbye to the people who once seemed so foreign and now are so utterly familiar. My last days in the village were amazing. Although I always knew the people in Mahon liked me well enough, their warm words and gestures over the past week were unbelievably touching. Aside from imploring me to stay on and promising to do their best to find me an African husband, they showered me with thanks, blessings, tons and tons of peanuts, and five chickens! (My neighbor wanted to give me a goat and seemed genuinely disappointed when I explained there was no way I could transport a goat to the United States, let alone to the capital of Burkina.) Although no official announcement had been made, somehow the entire village seemed to know I was leaving soon, and thus I spent the better part of the week repeating *"Amina"* (the traditional response meaning "Amen") to such benedictions as: "May God bless your parents for giving birth to you," and "May God keep you in good health and give you many children." The villagers' concern and well-wishes for my family—people they had never even met—only underscored the warmth and hospitality for which the Burkinabè people are known. Aside from the constant benedictions, the villagers also had a request for me: *Il ne faut pas nous oublier*.... Quite simply, "Don't forget us." For me, this was a request that was impossible to respond to; I did not know how to find the words to make them understand that I could never forget them or their kindness—that these people will always have a special place in my heart for opening up their village and their customs to me.

My last night in Mahon, the village threw an all-night party for me outside my house. Celebrations that lasted until the wee hours of the morning were the norm in Mahon, and my closest friends knew that I had never quite mustered the stamina for these events and was usually in bed fairly early. But in the days leading up to the party, I was told, "You are not going to get to go to sleep this night!" And they were nearly right. For hours, we danced under an African sky full of stars as the local *balafon* (traditional xylophone) players performed their music. Later, the theater group I had worked so hard to establish staged their skits for the crowd. People kept asking me to get out my camera and take photos, but I politely refused. I kept saying it was too dark for photos and, although it was, the real reason was that I knew pictures would never adequately capture the scene in front of me, nevermind all the emotions I was feeling. I closed my eyes and took a series of mental snapshots: the musicians' hands moving furiously upon their instruments, the circular conga-like line snaking around me, and the children on the edge of the crowd giddily playing tag the way any kids in America would.

The next morning, I awoke after a few hours of sleep. Mahon was quiet. I had never once been awake before the villagers (or the roosters), but this time, all was silent as I put the last of my things together and I looked around my little house. Soon, a small crowd had formed outside, and 35 people escorted me to wait for the bus. When the bus pulled up, I was surprised by my own emotions. During their two years of service, there are certainly many moments when Volunteers fantasize about going home, about finishing service and saying, "I am done!" But now that the moment was finally here, the reality that I may never see these people again was difficult to take.

The Burkinabè have an interesting custom for goodbyes. When you leave to go on a long journey, you must shake hands with the left hand. This is quite significant because normally doing anything with your left hand is culturally inappropriate and is actually quite rude. But the custom holds that now you must shake hands with your left because it indicates that you have to return at some point to rectify this wrong. As the bus pulled up, my friend Clarisse held out her left hand for me to shake. I felt as if I had been stabbed as it finally sunk in that this was really goodbye. This gesture was repeated over and over during a cacophony of even more benedictions, more "Aminas," more pleas not to forget the people of the village, and mostly, my own repeating of *"A ni ce kossbe...a ni ce...a ni ce."* (Thank you for everything...thank you.) The bus driver finally honked that it was time for me to board. By the time I had said my last goodbyes and managed to load my things—chickens and all—on the bus, I was quite a sight. Despite the fact that I had worked hard during my two years to understand and adapt to local customs, this morning I couldn't help but break some of the rules. People in Burkina Faso do not cry in public. Yet, here I was, walking onto a bus crowded with startled, staring African passengers, crying like a baby.

Now that my Volunteer service has ended, people ask me if I think I have changed because of this experience. I may still be too close to the experience to tell. But there are little things I've noticed: I've gained a good deal more patience, I've lost a certain sense of vanity, and I've dis-

> *I think I've learned less about me and more about the human condition.*

covered the joys of eating with my hands and bathing under the stars. In general, however, I think I've learned less about me and more about the human condition. Burkina Faso is a terribly impoverished country and the substandards of living, particularly *en brousse* (in the bush), are something we as Americans could never fully understand. This is a country with more than 50 ethnic groups and languages, let alone a belief in magic and ritual that doesn't easily fit into our Western logic. But what I have learned is that, despite all of this, the Burkinabè are not so different from us. Babies get born, children grow up, marriages take place, people die. People fight, love each other, develop friendships, have enemies. Some people work hard, some people don't. And at night, people go to bed only to get up the next morning to do it all again. We go through this life with its good days and its bad days and, ultimately, it is our relationships with others that make all the difference. The beauty of the Peace Corps, of this experience, is realizing that I have much more in common with a group of African villagers than I ever thought possible. John F. Kennedy, in creating the Peace Corps, said one of its goals would be to foster a cultural understanding between peoples all over the world. To me, that goal, beyond any work I did in Burkina Faso, is the one I am most proud to have achieved.

Caroline Chambre served as a community health development Volunteer in Burkina Faso from 2002 to 2004. Her work included improving the capacity of her village's health dispensary and collaborating with community groups to promote health education and awareness. A graduate of the University of North Carolina with a joint B.A. degree in English and French, she joined the Peace Corps after working in the nonprofit sector. Caroline returned to the United States to pursue a master's degree in international nonprofit and public management at New York University.

Taking Time
Walter Hawkes • Tanzania

"You should do very well as a Peace Corps Volunteer. You're creative, and you have a solid entrepreneurial background," offered one of my dad's friends, a successful businessman, in response to my impending departure for service in Tanzania, East Africa.

"Thanks, I hope so. I really would like to make a difference."

And so do most Volunteers as they set out, I thought, somewhat naively. At the date of official conscription, my wife and I boarded a plane bound for destinations unknown to us; I was to serve as an information technology (IT) Volunteer, and she was to be a biology and health Volunteer.

As part of pre-service training, the six IT Volunteers were assigned to internship schools. We were warned that, although each internship school would have computers, we were not to expect too much, as computers were still very new to Tanzania. I was assigned to Arusha Secondary School and would be the sole IT Volunteer placed there.

As I was led into the computer lab for the first time on the first morning, I steeled myself in anticipation of finding a cobweb-infested computer graveyard. But to my surprise, I saw six, four-year-old laptop computers. They weren't bad either, having been recently acquired and refurbished. The week was going to be easier than I had thought.

In the lab I was introduced to Agnes, a young Tanzanian woman who had been hired to train teachers at the school in computer literacy. Agnes was very cordial and friendly. Even better, she spoke English and would be my counterpart for the week. Chatting with Agnes, while examining the computers we'd be working with, I quickly learned that she had a decent general knowledge of computers and was probably quite adept at teaching Microsoft Office applications. I thought to myself that this was going to be a breeze. We'd probably be able to teach the teachers most of Word, Excel, and possibly Access. The setup was accommodating, and I was excited.

Reality set in, however, when the teachers, mostly middle-aged or older, entered the room. I greeted them enthusiastically in Kiswahili as they made their way to the computers. Most of them looked at me strangely, probably wondering why a foreigner was in their computer lab. They returned my greetings with somewhat less enthusiasm. After they had taken their seats at the computers, Agnes introduced me as an American who would be with them for a week to help teach computers. Agnes then commenced with a basic Microsoft Word lesson. She handed them each an exercise to complete, which consisted mostly of typing some text and then formatting it by changing the font, making it bold, etc. The teachers began working on the exercise while Agnes went around the room supervising, correcting, and teaching—all in Kiswahili. I watched closely as to how she was helping and, after a few minutes, I figured I could jump right in and make myself available to answer questions. One teacher turned to gain Agnes's attention. *"Mwalimu,"* she said. I quickly understood the word for teacher, so I approached.

"Can I help?" I asked in English.

"Mwalimu," she repeated, pointing at Agnes.

"I can answer questions."

"Mwalimu."

"Okay," I stammered while retreating, confused as to why she didn't want my help. After all, I didn't speak that much Kiswahili, but that shouldn't matter. They have to know English to be able to teach it. Besides, English is the official medium of instruction in all secondary schools in Tanzania.

Agnes finally explained to the woman the concept of selecting text, which had previously baffled her. When the teacher was satisfied, Agnes attended to the next person who needed assistance. Perhaps that was just the personality of the person wanting help. Maybe others would be grateful for my assistance.

Across the room I noticed two teachers trying their best to correct the grammar of a simple English sentence. They went back and forth, both offering options. Here's my chance, a nice teaching opportunity, I thought as I approached. "Hi," I said. "Actually neither of these is correct. You can write it this way..." I offered, unsolicited as it were, two ways to fix the broken, but trivial sentence. The two teachers listened, gawking at me as if soaking up my profound knowledge of the English language. Or so I thought. When I had finished, they said nothing and went back to arguing, in Kiswahili, over the same points they had been arguing prior to my intervention. I hadn't made a dent; I wasn't even heard.

After several similar instances, I became frustrated. Very frustrated. This is trivial subject material, what is the problem? Severe thoughts streamed to the forefront of my consciousness. Had I made a mistake in coming to Africa? How will I make a difference if no one here will listen to me?

Then Agnes announced that class was over; it was time for chai. I had tried several times to help and had been rebuffed, sometimes not so gently, in each of my attempts to teach, to help. I had failed miserably. Walking with Agnes, I broached my observations and frustrations. "Um, I'm not sure I'll be of much help this week, the teachers really don't seem to want to listen to me."

"Hakuna matata," she offered, telling me not to worry.

I tried again to gain some insight from Agnes, forging my statement into a more direct interrogatory. Again she replied, "Hakuna matata."

I remained unsuccessful in drawing any more information out of Agnes on what I thought was the more pertinent subject at hand. Instead we entered the staff lounge talking about food.

"Do you like *ugali*?" She inquired about a native dish.

"A little."

I glanced around the staff lounge and took note of some of the faces that looked familiar, a couple of my Volunteer friends and all of the teachers who had just been in the computer lab. They had made their way to the lounge for chai. I became a little uncomfortable, a little nervous. Perhaps they were not particularly thrilled to have us there. But my feelings quickly changed. Agnes led me over to a table where one of the women who hadn't listened to a single one of my English suggestions poured me a cup of chai and started chatting with me in Kiswahili.

"Habari za leo?" She inquired.

"My day is fine."

"Unatoka wapi?"

"I'm from America."

"Karibu sana!" (You are welcome here!)

"Asante sana" (Thank you very much) I said, appreciating the warm welcome.

We continued chatting for a few minutes, as much as I could in Kiswahili with only a few weeks of language training. She was very friendly and social, curious even. Her true personality was quite the opposite of my first impression. In fact, most of the people from the computer lab came to chat with me at some point during that chai break, and each subsequent one, with genuine hospitality. The teachers became more comfortable with me when they heard that I could speak some Kiswahili, or that I was expending effort in an attempt to speak it.

Curiously, the second trip to the computer lab, for the afternoon session with the same teachers, was far different from the first. Near the beginning, two teachers actually wanted my assistance and listened intently to what I told them. I would have never guessed that teaching something as trivial as how to bold text would come to feel like a success after such miserable failure. But it did, although it baffled me. Why did they want my help now, when they could not have been bothered in the morning? What had changed? I had only talked with them a little in the best Kiswahili I could muster, very little as it were, over a cup of chai. Surely something so simple could not possibly be the difference. Or could it?

> *This was great; I was really starting to help.*

The first night I went home, exhausted, of course, and learned as many new computer-related words in Kiswahili as I could. It helped. The next day in class, the more I attempted to provide assistance in my best, broken Kiswahili, the more people wanted my help. This was great; I was really starting to help. And I did something else. I never missed a visit to the staff lounge for a cup of chai and conversation. Again, the more I spoke informally with the teachers, the more they would listen to me and, in fact, seek out my assistance.

I eventually came to call this informal time we spent together "taking time." It's taking time to learn about teachers, students, colleagues, community members, their families, work, ideas, and passions. It's taking time to understand them, to become friendly with them, to care about them. For each of them matched my curiosity and care with their own, whether by cordially offering a cup of chai or by offering something more profound like genuine friendship. By the end of the week, one by one, all of the teachers had opened up to me and let me help them. I wasn't teaching them anything complicated, just simple concepts on the computer. But nonetheless, I felt good about it. The last day, when Agnes observed that I was as busy as she was, she caught my attention with a knowing glance and casually offered, "See? Hakuna matata." I smiled, and replied to her wise words from the first day, "You were right, there are no worries."

Prior to this experience, I had been blinded by my haste, my unrealistic expectations, and my desire to jump in head-first in an effort to move quickly and make as much difference as possible. There seems to be an unending number of intangibles in trying to make a difference here. The cultural divide alone is wide and complicated. Sometimes I feel lost at the start of a project, in trying to contemplate how it will eventually be accomplished and by what means. I'm feeling this now with the current seemingly insurmountable challenge I face. Almost 1,000 teacher trainees and staff members are waiting patiently for computer training at my permanent placement site at the Teachers Training College of Korogwe. Somehow this needs to be accomplished using the college's eight old, barely functioning computers. I haven't the foggiest notion how this will happen, but I do know one thing: the simple but previously confounding first step—taking time.

Walter Hawkes and his wife, Melinda, served as Volunteers in Tanzania from 2003 to 2004. They joined the Peace Corps following careers in technology and teaching. Upon their return, they moved to Los Angeles to pursue an interest in writing and filmmaking.

The Importance of Drinking Tea

Jake Jones • Morocco

Morocco is a country to be explored—as if by design. The number of hidden corners; the amount of diversity; the culture of hospitality and community; and the strong, continually changing landscape all desire to be discovered and studied. While I thought that my village was at the extreme edges of both isolation and charm, there was always one more hidden corner, one more isolated valley, one more rugged hillside that was more diverse, more distant, more alluring. So, when I could, I always took the opportunity to travel.

The regional trachoma drive gave me a regular opportunity to travel to even more remote villages. Trachoma is a contagious eye disease, usually spread by flies, that causes blindness if left untreated. Prevention is simple with basic improvements in sanitation, usually by removing areas that gather flies. The Moroccan government had instituted a program to saturate the affected areas with treatment and awareness-raising education.

I would join the Jeep full of local doctors and nurses and we would go jarring along a road that wasn't really a road to the distant settlements, villages, and nomadic tents of the region. We would set out early in the morning and return hot and tired at night. It would often take two or three days to cover the whole region. The same process was used for the quarterly vaccine drives.

One site was inaccessible by car. We parked next to a sandy, brown

> *Before the actual work began, we always had at least one glass of mint tea with some conversation about the local goings-on.*

hill and hiked 20 minutes on a high path above a river to descend into a wonderful green valley. Another site was a nomadic tent far in the desert, far from even the nearest village. Carpets were laid for us on the sandy ground to rest in the shade of the tent after we'd finished working.

Since there was no health facility in these communities, we sometimes worked from the local sheikh's house. We almost always began the visit with some mint tea, poured in an elaborate ceremony. The villagers came to receive their medication and instructions, along with a bit of socializing. Then we would be served couscous, eaten from a communal plate with our hands, followed by another round of mint tea.

This process was generally followed in every community we visited. Before the actual work began, we always had at least one glass of mint tea with some conversation about the local goings-on, regional events, and how everyone was doing. Then, after the work was finished, we generally had another glass of tea, some more conversation, then we were off to the next community.

It seemed to me that we could get much more work done if we refused the tea. In fact, we might be able to get to all of the communities in a single day. We didn't need to be rude, just a polite, "No, thanks; we have a lot of stops today" should do it.

"Jake, sit down and drink your tea. The villagers aren't even here yet; they just learned that we arrived." Sometimes I just received an impatient sign to sit down and not worry.

At one stop, a few houses were nestled in the side of a rocky hillside surrounded by small herds of goats scraping for what greenery there was to eat. I was delighted to see a generator-powered television and the host served us warm soda instead of tea. As I drank my soda and squinted into the fuzzy green TV screen, I became aware of the silence around me. Our host was sleeping; the rest of the household was trying to watch the television program, just like me.

I quickly realized an important aspect of our visit was gone. While the work was done in short order, there was no real connection between this community and us. I had been complaining about drinking tea before and after our work, but I saw that it helped establish respect and connection in each community we visited. I still have no other memory of that village; I don't even remember its name. I only recall that TV screen and the sleeping host.

As we got up and reloaded the Jeep, our host gave us a sleepy goodbye and, rather than try to hurry home, I started to look forward to my next glass of mint tea and lively local gossip.

Jake Jones originally served in Uzbekistan as a maternal and child health Volunteer in 2001. Later he served in Morocco as a water and sanitation Volunteer. Jake then joined the first group of Volunteers in Azerbaijan, completing his Peace Corps service in December 2005.

Been There, Done That
Stephanie Saltzman · Zambia

y friends always ask me to write a story about my Peace Corps experiences. I have always refused because I don't have the words to capture all the emotions, experiences, and life changes that come with being a Volunteer who served in three African countries. There simply is not one story that captures the feelings of despair followed by elation, of hopelessness followed by optimism, of self doubt followed by satisfaction of a job well done. How can someone who hasn't "been there, done that" understand my love of the rural African village and my desire to go back to be a part of the African village life? Or how much I miss sitting on my back steps with my neighbor's children eating fresh-picked bananas? Or how deeply I was touched by my next-door neighbors who, even as they struggled to support themselves, invited me for dinner every night to share what little food they had? Or appreciate all the experiences that went into my work as a small business development Volunteer in Africa?

I began my Peace Corps service as a Volunteer in Uganda and Kenya. I returned home for a couple of years to work and to pursue a master's degree, yet Africa continued to call to me. So when the opportunity arose to go back to Africa as a Peace Corps Crisis Corps Volunteer* in Zambia for six months working on an HIV/AIDS project, I jumped at

*Peace Corps Response, formerly known as Crisis Corps, offers Volunteers an opportunity to return to the field in short-term, high inpact assignments that typically range from three to six months.

> *I had learned from my earlier experiences as a Volunteer that taking a step back and evaluating was never a bad thing.*

the chance. After all, I knew what it was like to live without electricity and running water, I knew how to use a pit latrine, and even to crave foods I never thought I would eat. I'd "been there, done that."

My job was to evaluate the micro-credit program of a local nongovernmental organization (NGO) called Harvest Help, which had an HIV/AIDS project in a district in Zambia. Harvest Help had obtained funding to give loans to women's groups whose members were being affected by the HIV/AIDS pandemic. Because HIV/AIDS affects these women on a daily basis, it is important for their survival and all the people who depend on them to help create viable businesses and give them the skills to sustain those businesses. Though the NGO had successfully distributed the grant monies, it was having difficulty getting the groups to repay the loans. Many of the small businesses had failed.

I had learned from my earlier experiences as a Volunteer that taking a step back and evaluating was never a bad thing. So when I first arrived, I spent time assessing the different groups. Harvest Help's staff wanted me to focus on business management training-of-trainers because that is where they thought they needed the most help. But I needed to look at the whole program—from start to finish—to see how it was being run.

In one instance, I learned that the NGO had paid for two knitting machines for a women's group from Chirundu to make sweaters and sell them. Unfortunately, no one had considered that Chirundu was one of the hottest places in Zambia. When I went one Wednesday to visit this women's group, they proudly informed me that they already had business training. Then I found out this "business training" consisted only of learning how to fill out a record sheet and monitor time worked. When I asked about a business plan and a group constitution, there was no reply. So we started from the beginning, discussing the group and its objectives and how a business would fit in with those objectives.

As we were discussing types of businesses and considerations for choosing a business, the women realized that choosing the right business and planning for it can mean its success or failure. Hence the need for a business plan as part of the application process—not just to assess a group's business, but to make sure members have thought through their ideas. This is especially important in an environment where people often choose a business simply by looking at what other businesses are around and deciding to go into one of those businesses.

When I discussed the lack of business planning with my counterparts at Harvest Help, they told me that the criteria for loans in the past had been partially based on need and, of course, with the HIV/AIDS pandemic, there is always need. From a purely business perspective, however, need alone does not make a business plan. That doesn't mean that people in need cannot run a great business.

Once my counterparts realized the necessity of a structured process, it was not difficult to start organizing the loan program. We crafted a policy that would determine eligibility for the program, ensuring that the monies would go to the intended recipients. We created a basic application packet that included a loan application, a group constitution, and a basic business plan—all translated into the local language. Even though I had been teaching business practices throughout this process, Harvest Help now had the foundation necessary for its loan program to be sustainable.

Toward the end of my six months, I did another two-day business training in a very rural area. It was so rural, in fact, that we had to take a boat to get there because the roads were nearly impassable. During the group introduction, I realized the group had been in existence for a year, but had no mission statement. Members could not tell me definitively why they were in existence and what their purpose was. So, before I could lead any business training, we worked on group capacity-building. We spent time defining the group's goals and mission statement, writing up bylaws, and doing some action planning. Only then could I return to my planned agenda and start what I'd set out to do—teach the group about building up a business.

As a Volunteer, I came to learn that you can plan and plan and sometimes things would work out accordingly, but more often than not, you just had to be flexible. Though there were many digressions from our original plans, in the end, we still reached our goals more often than not. Had I not "been there, done that," I wouldn't have all the experiences, memories, and emotions that have left me with too many stories to tell and not enough words to tell them.

Stephanie Saltzman served as a Peace Corps Volunteer working in small enterprise development in Uganda and Kenya from 1998 to 2000. She also served as a Peace Corps Crisis Corps Volunteer working on HIV/AIDS initiatives in Zambia from October 2003 to March 2004. She returned to the U.S. to work at Peace Corps headquarters.

Itam

Jeff Fearnside · Kazakhstan

I met him when he came to pick me up from the Sovietera sanatorium, where I had spent my first three days in Kazakhstan learning as quickly as possible some of the complexities of this vast country. I hadn't known a word in Russian before I arrived, and I struggled to properly pronounce my simple greeting to him and his wife, Farida.

"Zdravstvuite, menya zovut Jeff." (Hello, my name is Jeff.)

They both smiled politely and introduced themselves, but said nothing more.

It was early June, but already hot. The ride to my new home, a village on the edge of the foothills of the snow-peaked Tian Shan (Celestial Mountains), took two hours. Along the way, Farida stopped to do some shopping. While we waited, Itam played a battered tape of ethnic Uighur music, which I liked.

Here we first used the goulash of languages that would see us through the next two and a half months of my training—a mix of Russian, English, German, and gestures. Itam had studied German at a university many years earlier, and I had taken a semester of it nearly as long ago. He had picked up some English from his two sons who were studying it, while I took Russian lessons every day.

He always spoke slowly and clearly to me in Russian, which I appreciated. But, like many people, he also had the habit of speaking extremely loud, as if sheer volume would somehow help me understand better.

"Jeffrey, come!" he boomed at mealtimes, his light green eyes laughing. *"Kushai, kushai!"* It would become a familiar refrain—eat, eat!—along with *chai pit* (drink tea) and *chutchut*. Literally, this means "a little," but in Kazakhstan there's no such thing as a little when it comes to food or drink. Though Kazakhstan is a Muslim country, much of the population drinks, perhaps a holdover from Soviet times. While Itam occasionally enjoyed vodka, he did so moderately, and he never pressured me to join him.

I called him my host father, but he was only eight years older than me, so he was really more like a protective older brother. He taught me the finer points about local customs, gently chiding me for shaking water from my hands after I washed them (Uighurs believe this brings misfortune) and showing me how to give handshakes the Central Asian way—lightly but warmly, with free hands holding each other's forearms to show respect.

When I discovered that I had forgotten to bring a handkerchief with me, he gave me one of his. In every way, he made a special effort to include me in his life and the life of his family.

"Jeffrey!" he boomed. "You, me, go *arbeiten*." He always used the German word for "to work," though I understood the Russian—*rabotat*—just as well. He was a veterinarian, and I would watch as he peered into cows' eyes, administered shots, and rubbed ointment into their sores.

Another time, he and Farida had me dress in my best for an Uighur wedding.

Ethnic Uighurs trace their roots to the primarily Muslim Xinjiang province of China and are closely related to the Turkic people of Central Asia. This wedding featured some folk music similar to what I had heard on my first ride with Itam. They also played Russian rock 'n' roll and, more than once, the extended live version of the Eagles' "Hotel California."

At first, I felt shy and resisted invitations to join in the dancing. I sat on the periphery and watched, enjoying the seemingly bottomless portions of salads and appetizers that were a meal to me, though they were really just the warm-up to the actual meal. Eventually, I was moved to join the happy throng, the men in suits, the women in glittering dresses, their arms gracefully twining and untwining above their heads. We danced all through the evening and into the next morning.

> *It's funny how small, seemingly insignificant moments in our lives can take on such meaning later.*

The days moved slowly that summer in my village. It wasn't exactly a place that time had passed by, but certainly only fingers of modernity had managed to slip in under the blanket of time. My family had electricity and a television, but, like most of their fellow villagers, no telephone. Water had to be carried from a well half a kilometer away; hot water was made by boiling it or, for outdoor showers, leaving a barrel exposed to the sun all day.

The family's fortune, if counted in hard currency, was a trifle. Itam's income barely met their needs. But, as with Central Asian peoples since before recorded history, their real wealth was measured in the richness of their family life and in animals—in their case, sheep.

Toward the end of my stay, they needed to sell five sheep from their flock to pay for their children's education for the coming year. I was invited along to help catch them. We hopped onto a small horse-drawn cart and slowly clopped up the road to the pasture where two *pastukhi*, or shepherds, were overseeing the common herd. Itam's father-in-law chose the best from among them. Itam, his sons, and I chased them down, tied them up, and placed them in the cart.

Clouds of dust rose into the sky, the sun fell toward the horizon, and the nearby mountains faded into a hazy blue and then an indistinct shadow. It was dark when we rode back down the road toward home. I felt bad for the poor sheep lying next to me, but I felt good knowing that we were taking part in a cycle of life that had been played out for centuries here—knowing that Malik and Adik would be able to continue studying English, that Takmina would gain a marketable skill in learning to cut and style hair before eventually going on to a university as well.

I also sensed that Itam was proud of me for helping his family in this way. My feeling of this only increased on his 45th birthday, the first and only time I ever saw him drunk.

He came in late for dinner, having been out celebrating with two friends from his university days. While Farida ladled out soup and prepared a pot of strong black tea, Itam rambled on, more emotional than usual. His family, unaccustomed to this, largely remained quiet. Finally, he put down his spoon and looked directly at me, struggling for words.

"Moe serdtse..." he said at last, pressing his hand to his chest. When I said I didn't understand, he repeated it in English.

"My... my heart...."

I was touched. He was trying to tell me how much he would miss me. I placed my hand on his forearm and squeezed.

My training was over, and the time to leave for my assignment as a full-fledged Volunteer had arrived. All the family came to see me off, all except for Itam. He had planned his vacation for this time and was away again with his university friends.

I tried to give back Itam's handkerchief, but Farida refused, saying that I would need it. She also promised that Itam would meet me at the train station.

To my disappointment, he never showed up. But I left with hugs from the rest of the family and more memories than it seemed two and a half months could possibly provide.

After a 15-hour train ride, I arrived at my new home, Shymkent. Far from being the dangerous place I had been warned about ("Texas" my host family called it, for they believed it was like the Wild West), I found this sprawling, low-rise city colorful and friendly. Its tree-lined streets were cool and dotted with many interesting ethnic cafes. The university where I would teach was small, but its students were enthusiastic. I looked forward to a bright two years of work.

This exciting time was darkened by some terrible news: Itam had died the day after I left. Previously unknown to everyone, he'd had a heart condition, which became lethal when combined with his recent celebrations.

I remembered him talking of his heart and was shocked to realize he had been trying to tell us of feeling pains in his chest. In hindsight, it seems we might have caught this, but at the time it was the farthest notion from our minds. He was middle-aged and seemingly in perfect health. Only days before I had wrestled sheep to the ground with him.

I learned another hard lesson in hindsight when I found that I didn't have a single photograph of Itam. I had photos of the rest of the family, my Peace Corps friends, some village children, my pupils, even a few random pastukhi. I must have assumed that Itam would always be around, that I would have plenty of chances to catch him at just the right moment.

The only tangible remembrance I had was his handkerchief.

It's funny how small, seemingly insignificant moments in our lives can take on such meaning later. If I had brought a handkerchief with me to Kazakhstan, then I would have nothing to remember Itam by.

There's nothing obviously extraordinary about it. It's just a simple piece of cloth, probably bought at the local bazaar for a few *tenge* coins. Yet, when I look at it, I see pictures woven into the cotton: I see laughing light green eyes and, in them, the reflection of lush green foothills, snow-peaked mountains, dusty pastures, hazy steppe sunsets. And darkness. But in that darkness rings the clip-clop of horse hooves, the trill of Uighur wedding music, a voice booming "Jeffrey!" and I feel that at any moment I might stand up and dance.

Jeff Fearnside served in the Peace Corps as a university instructor teaching English as a foreign language in Kazakhstan from 2002 to 2004. His short stories, poems, and essays have appeared in Aethlon, Isotope, Permafrost, Rock & Sling, *and the anthology,* Scent of Cedars: Promising Writers of the Pacific Northwest.

Leave Taking

Beth Genovese · Panama

A rriving at Rio Oeste Arriba (West River Above) in Panama re-quired walking 45 minutes down from the main road that runs through the province of Bocas del Toro. The community of Rio Oeste has 500 Ngobe indigenous people. Half of them lived in the center of the community, which was anchored by *La Iglesia de Cristo* (the Church of Christ). The other half chose to live farther out, close to the land they worked to produce root vegetables for consumption and plantains and cocoa for income. For the last seven months of my two-year service, I visited and worked regularly with 12 families in Rio Oeste on projects ranging from business education to conservation.

Cata was the head of one of these families. She had 10 children and, like most Ngobe women, she was short and thick. She wore her long black hair pulled tightly into a braided ponytail. She had never cut her hair; doing so was considered bad luck. She had wise, sad eyes buried by a heavy, round face. Her unusually strong personality and sharp tongue were softened only slightly by her smile.

I visited Cata almost every Sunday, and we would talk and laugh as she completed one of her many household chores. The last Sunday I spent in Rio Oeste, Cata told me she wanted to show me parts of the river I had never seen. Dreading a long day of visitors and quiet goodbyes, the walk sounded like a good escape.

We set out at 7:00 a.m.—Cata was always prompt—with her son

> *I was guilty of playing favorites among the community kids, and often paid Iscar special attention.*

Gadiel and his friend, both in their 20s, and her younger, 12-year-old son, Iscar, who was more commonly known by his nickname, Mudo. When he was a baby, meningitis had left him deaf. Although he was capable of making sounds, Panamanians generally do not distinguish between the deaf and mute, so he was labeled with the nickname *mudo*, which means mute.

I was guilty of playing favorites among the community kids, and often paid Iscar special attention. I loved him for his expressiveness—loud in its silence and insistence. Whenever I walked through the village, he would suddenly materialize at my side. Smiling, he would tentatively grab my hand, squeeze it and let go—a release that always came too quickly for me. Hungry for praise, Iscar often appeared at my door to show me the grades in his school notebooks. Educating him was complex. Iscar was forever in elementary school because the second-grade teacher, a gentle woman who had taught in the community for over 20 years, was the only teacher in the school patient enough to find new ways to teach him. Although Iscar was practically crippled by meningitis as a baby, Cata had devised her own physical therapy routine, and he had grown remarkably strong. Often, I would see this boy who couldn't have weighed more than 70 pounds scrambling down from the mountain, hauling on his back 50-pound sacks of plantains.

Toward the end of our walk by the river, Cata and I sat on a ledge of rocks overlooking the water. The boys stripped down to their shorts and dove in, and Cata began to talk. The conversation meandered until she suddenly settled on the real purpose of our walk.

She turned to face me. *"Puedes llevar Mudo contigo?"* she asked. (Can you take Mudo with you?)

I wasn't wholly surprised by her question. I had noted that Iscar was dressed in his nicer clothes, and I had been asked half-seriously by more casual acquaintances to take their children and teach them English, to make them *gringos*. Still, I had not fully anticipated this request from Cata. Wary I might be translating in error, I asked her for clarification—would I, or could I?

"Los dos," she replied. (Both.)

"Technically," I said, weighing my words carefully, "it would be possible, but I would have to adopt him legally."

"Está bien." she said. (It's OK.)

So, yes, I could do it. But would I? *"Yo no se,"* I said slowly. (I don't know.)

I was looking steadily at her, but I was thinking about the challenges I would face returning home after two years away. And, until I settled on a career plan, I would have little financial stability. Why couldn't I just say no?

Eager to change the focus of our conversation, I smiled and asked if she wouldn't miss him terribly if she sent him away with me.

"Sì, claro," she replied. (Of course.) "But I know he would be safe with you; I know how much you care for him. You know he is intelligent. If he stays here, he will be in our house forever. We can't afford to send him to a special school, he will never learn more than what he knows now, and he will have no opportunities. The people here will only ever see him as Mudo."

I sat very still, quiet and pensive. With my knees to my chest, I looked at my feet. I could not take Iscar with me. Employing humor, a form of communication we were both comfortable with, I told Cata I wasn't prepared to be responsible for a child fresh out of the jungle with special needs and besides, Iscar would not fit inside my backpack. Although we both laughed at the image, I felt only pain because I did not have the capacity to help this child.

I knew Iscar was intelligent and curious and with opportunity he would learn and perhaps flourish. I wanted to give him this opportunity, but I felt there were limits to what I could do, and I wasn't sure that removing Iscar from his home, his family, and his culture was truly a so-

> *I realized that my work wasn't about directly creating change, but motivating change in others.*

lution. My experience in the Peace Corps had taught me that even some of the most straightforward challenges are, paradoxically, complex.

But I didn't have to explain this to Cata. She reached out, touched my arm and asked why I wasn't swimming. I stood and wiped away the tears that rimmed my eyes, shucked my black rubber swamp boots, peeled off my sweaty socks and dove into the water after Iscar. I signaled him to race me to the far side of the slow-moving river. He beat me by two full strokes and looked back grinning.

I have been home now for five months. Like Iscar letting go of my hand, the release from Panama came a little too quickly. I still feel overwhelmed with emotion when I look through the stacks of photos I have from Rio Oeste. I have told Iscar's story more than once and inevitably someone asks why I didn't bring him home. The question frustrates me until I remember that I would have asked the same question before I served in the Peace Corps. It took me many months before I realized that my work in Panama wasn't about directly creating change, but motivating change in others.

When I left Rio Oeste, the pastor thanked me for caring for Iscar and the other children. He told me that of all the work I had done in the community, the most important was reminding them that their children are their best resource. I left hoping that I motivated change in perception, in treatment, in priorities. And I settled for taking Iscar, Cata, and Rio Oeste home only in my heart.

Beth Genovese served as a business development Volunteer in Panama from 2002 to 2004. She joined the Peace Corps following a career working in various areas of small business development. Upon her return, Beth consulted for small businesses and pursued a master's degree in marriage and family therapy/art therapy.

Window
to the World

"The Peace Corps opens
a window to the world
for many people. I went
through that window
and became president
of my country."

*Former President
Alejandro Toledo
Peru*

Harvesting Friendship
Kay Oursler • Tanzania

As a Volunteer doing environmental work, I planted a lot of seeds during 31 months of service. However, the majority of those seeds never saw soil. Rather, they were planted in the minds and hearts of the people in a small village in Tanzania. I lived in Uhekule, at the foothills of the Kipengere Mountain Range, about a 12-hour bus ride from Dar es Salaam—Tanzania's largest city and commercial capital. Nearly two hours away is Njombe, the closest town with electricity.

HIV/AIDS is a problem throughout Tanzania and became the focal point of several of my Peace Corps projects in my village. One project continues to be an integral part of my life now that I am back in the States, the genesis of which was a seed planted in my heart.

One day I saw Isaya, an 11-year-old boy, selling onions on the side of the street. I asked him why he wasn't in school and he said his parents had died and he had to sell the onions to feed himself. That's when I heard a higher voice telling me to one day build an orphanage. At that time, there were 114 orphans in my village of 1,450 and the majority of their parents had died from AIDS. Such an orphanage remains a goal for my post-Peace Corps service. I am raising money to begin construction on a building in the coming year. This interest to continue a connection with the people I worked with and care about is something many returned Volunteers have.

But I'm jumping ahead in my story, which included many great moments. One of those moments occurred when several young women showed up to work in a community garden I had started for those suffering from HIV. Previously, I told a man in the village the garden was for sick people, asking him, "Where are all the women with HIV?" He said they were afraid to be seen in public. Then one day, after word of the garden had spread, 10 mothers with HIV came into my yard with buckets of compost on their heads, ready to work in the garden. I fought back tears, realizing the strength it took for those women to leave their homes and participate. I introduced them to green beans. They hadn't realized they could eat the exterior of a bean and I taught them how to prepare them. They had also never had broccoli or leaf lettuce. The women learned about nutrition and would talk and laugh together. It became a wonderful garden that saw all of us experience more than just the growth of plants.

Another enterprising group of women benefited from a jam project we began during my first year in Tanzania. I used to make jelly with my mother for years and decided to form a Mama's group for jam making. In my village, I saw a lot of rhubarb and I told the women, "We should make jam out of that." They insisted we couldn't because it was just a flower, but I helped them see it differently and it would become our most popular jam. Nine of the women are still making jars of jam and shipping them to Dar es Salaam to be sold.

Such interaction with the women and others connected me to the community. Soon after my arrival I found myself writing a President's Emergency Plan for AIDS Relief (PEPFAR) grant for an HIV/AIDS seminar that included education and testing. I also oversaw a library project and the construction of a dispensary—just the second building in the village to have indoor plumbing.

All of this work, however, was secondary to the relationships I built.

My story is different from most Volunteers, as I entered the Peace Corps at age 65. After retirement in 2004, I found life to be filled with many activities but not enough substance. So, I fulfilled a dream I had 20 years ago, to serve in the Peace Corps.

> *Because I am older, I was treated with great respect, almost revered.*

I left my new and very lovely retirement home to begin two-plus years of the most rewarding and adventuresome time of my life. I didn't really know what to expect when I joined. As one of those "nontraditional" Volunteers well beyond her college years, I was the oldest Volunteer in my service group. It was sometimes frustrating to see the younger Volunteers pick up the language so easily. However, once I got placed in my village things got easier. While I still struggled with speaking Kiswahili, it provided fodder to banter with the kids, and I had picked up enough to feel comfortable. I immediately fell in love with the area and the people. There was no electricity and water was fetched from a distance, but I felt a peace I had never experienced before. Life was so simple. Because I am older, I was treated with great respect, almost revered.

During my first year I was both aided by, and able to assist, a young woman, Shukuru, whom I met through the head schoolmaster, Gabriel. Shukuru had been orphaned since she was 14 and had dropped out of school to care for three younger brothers. I asked Gabriel what the protocol was in order to employ Shukuru, now 18, to help me with my language and household chores. In a visit to her home I observed how little this orphaned family had—a dirt floor, no furniture, a piece of foam as beds, and only one blanket. Together, Gabriel and I asked her grandfather permission for Shukuru to work with me, which he granted.

After knowing one another for a year, I asked Shukuru if she wanted to go back to school and she got a big smile on her face. I reasoned, "You're smart enough to understand my Kiswahili so you can definitely go to school." She and her brothers are now all in boarding school. It has been my joy to help them in this way. I love Shukuru like my own daughter.

Such affection was returned threefold among the villagers, who held an elaborate farewell party as I ended my Peace Corps service.

They had planned the event for months, with various dignitaries, a guest speaker, dancing, and children singing songs in English. Their generosity included gifts of crafts and food.

There were 450 pounds of hand-shelled corn, 200 pounds of wheat, 48 handmade woven baskets, 15 large, woven mats, 7 woven handbags, 3 guinea pigs, 7 chickens, 27 eggs, 10 traditional Tanzanian *kangas* (skirts), and many African carvings.

Everything but a partridge in a pear tree!

I was so touched. Much of this, of course, I left for the village to use. Some items I shipped home to incorporate when sharing my stories about Tanzania.

It was difficult to leave behind such good friends and a community that had become a family, but I have plans to return in September of 2008 to pursue the orphanage project.

Which brings me to my family in America.

Another difficult part of being an older Volunteer has been convincing my two children, eight grandchildren and one great-grandchild that I can still be a mother and grandmother even though I'm a continent away.

My daughter-in-law says, "We have three children who need their grandmother." But I tell her this is my passion and my mission. Now they don't think I'll come back; that I'll stay in Tanzania.

To be honest, I just might. It's just such a simple life. I can live without electricity and running water. The orphanage project and HIV garden await me and I'm ready to plant some more seeds.

Kay Oursler served as an environment Volunteer in Tanzania from 2005 to 2007, joining the Peace Corps at the age of 65. She extended her original 27-month commitment by four months to complete a library and primary school project. A resident of Hot Springs Village, Arkansas, she is currently leading a fundraising campaign to build an orphanage in her former worksite, hoping to begin actual construction in the fall of 2008.

Enough Time

Diana Schmidt · Ukraine

I always believed there would be enough time.

In 1961, when the Peace Corps was a grand idea, maybe a little impractical, maybe overly idealistic, I believed there would be enough time.

Time to finish university studies, go on to graduate school, have a career or two, and even possibly raise a family. Plenty of time. Whenever the thought of joining Peace Corps came up, I'd think, "There will be enough time."

Then, on a lonely back road in southern France, I almost ran out of time. I still remember that day. It began with wind and rain and my desire to finish our bike trip, to get to the five-star hotel, have a shower and a celebratory dinner after nine strenuous days of biking the calm, quiet roads.

Late that afternoon, just a half hour away from that five-star hotel, a lone car came silently and swiftly behind us, pulled around Hugo, my husband, and suddenly cut back into our lane. Without warning, I flew into the air as if lifted by a giant, unseen hand. Coming down, I hit the car and then hit the road. Lying on the ground, I thought, "It would be so easy to die on this road." I thought of all I had accomplished, all the friends I had made, all I had seen of the world. I thought of how I had always believed that I had all the time in the world. And, I thought of how I had never joined the Peace Corps.

Hugo was lying on the road, holding me. I whispered to him, "If I survive, will you join the Peace Corps with me?" What could he say but, "Yes." The day ended with a promise. I would finally join the Peace Corps. There would be enough time.

But first I needed to recover from a broken left leg, sprained right ankle, broken pelvis, and dislocated shoulder. It took a year to heal and learn to walk again. As soon as I could walk, Hugo and I applied to Peace Corps and we were accepted as business development Volunteers, assigned to Ukraine in February 2000.

Recently someone asked me, "Lying on that road, why did you regret not joining the Peace Corps?" This is a complex question. Then and now, the Peace Corps represented to me the chance to make a positive difference in the world, to give back a little for the advantages I had enjoyed simply by being born an American. Joining the Peace Corps was also a promise I had made to myself when I was young, idealistic, and bold and I wanted to keep that promise and see myself as still being young, idealistic, and bold. But maybe my strongest reason for joining the Peace Corps was that I didn't want to die with any regrets.

After three months of training, Hugo and I were assigned to live and work in Nikolaev, a large, shipbuilding city in the south of Ukraine. During the Soviet times, Nikolaev was the "shipbuilding capital" of the Soviet Union and residents were still dreaming of those days of glory. As a "closed city," foreigners were not allowed to come to Nikolaev so Hugo and I stood out more than usual. It seemed as if every third person thought we were spies and the rest wondered what terrible thing we had done in the United States to get sent to Nikolaev to "volunteer."

My job, specifically, was to work at the Women's Business Center, helping unemployed women learn to start small businesses. Since I had been involved in the field of business in the United States for many years before coming to Ukraine, I naively thought, "Piece of cake." Little did I know when we arrived in Nikolaev that the basic concepts of profit, risk-reward, and planning were as foreign to the women I'd be working with as the concept of "communal services" was to me.

One day, I offered to teach a class in business planning. I wanted to make the concept easy to understand so I decided to use the metaphor of a "road trip." In a mixture of Russian and English, I bravely began. "Let's suppose you want

> *I realized that I was hooked on living a life that seemed full of meaning, challenge, and adventure.*

to drive your car from Nikolaev to Kyiv. How would you plan your trip?" I waited. No response. I waited. Still no response. So, I decided to get the conversation going. "Let's see," I said, "I guess the first thing I'd do is look at a map and pick the best route. Then, I'd decide how long it would take and make sure to leave early enough, bring along some food, fill the car with gas and other supplies. Then, I'd look at alternative routes, in case I ran into trouble along the way. For example, maybe one of the roads would be closed for repairs so I'd have to know an alternative route." All this time, I was pointing to the map, illustrating my points and writing the steps on the chalkboard.

Finally, Gallina spoke up. "How can you plan your trip this way? You might not have enough money, you might need to take care of your sick mother, your car might break down. It is better not to plan so much since you can't control the future. It is better just to set off when the time is right."

Olga added, "You Americans... you are always planning. You plan too much!"

I never did manage to convince most of the women I worked with that planning was a good idea. After all, they had experienced a life so much different from mine—a life that seemed to be, and was, completely out of their control, a life that had a whole different set of "rules" for survival, let alone success. But we did finally agree that making a profit was a good thing for a business and many of the women actually managed to not only open small businesses, but to make a profit and eventually grow their businesses and hire others to work for them.

> *I knew that I was making a difference in their lives. What I didn't realize, at the time, was how significant of a difference they were making in my life.*

When Hugo and I returned to our home in California after being Peace Corps Volunteers, I realized that I was hooked on living a life that seemed full of meaning, challenge, and adventure. Living in Ukraine was both a constant puzzle (How do I mail a package? How can I get flour and sugar from the corner market using only the Russian that I know?) and a chance to test my assumptions about life and the way the world "should" work (people should smile at strangers on the street, meetings should actually happen close to the agreed upon time, planning is a good thing). My work as a Volunteer helping unemployed women learn to start businesses was very fulfilling. I knew that I was making a difference in their lives. What I didn't realize, at the time, was how significant of a difference they were making in my life.

Returning home, we quickly picked up right where we left off, moved back into our house, bought a car, and picked up the dog. I even moved easily back into work. But life seemed pale and not so interesting. I knew without even thinking about it how to mail a package and how to buy food at the grocery store. And, no matter what work I did, I didn't seem to have the same sense of accomplishment.

I began to reason that if I actually worked for the Peace Corps, in a job supporting the work of many Volunteers, I could multiply my minor successes one-hundredfold. Instead of doing just what I could personally accomplish, I could leverage my earlier efforts. So, I turned to Hugo and said, once again, "Will you join Peace Corps with me?" With his agreement, I applied for a job, was accepted, and found myself back in Ukraine as the associate Peace Corps director and program and training officer. This time, Max, the dog, came with us. Six years later, after a stint in Macedonia as country director and returning to Ukraine as country director, I know that being run over by that car was one of the best things that ever happened to me.

And, I also know that I'm very, very glad there was enough time.

Diana Schmidt and her husband served in Ukraine from 2000 to 2001. Diana worked as a business development Volunteer. She became associate Peace Corps director and program and training officer in Ukraine and then country director in Macedonia in 2004. She has since returned to Ukraine as country director. Prior to the Peace Corps, Diana co-founded an ophthalmic pharmaceutical company in 1991. She holds a Ph.D. from the University of California and an M.B.A. from Pepperdine University.

If There's Enough for One

Kara Garbe · *Burkina Faso*

I didn't know what animal the head in my soup had come from. When Gara set the first bowl down beside the *forestier* (environmentalist), he pulled a slimy gray wad from an open cavern of bone, offering me first dibs on the brain. I shook my head in something approaching panic: me, the girl who was just easing away from seven years as a vegetarian. And while the forestier, the local government agent charged with enforcing environmental laws, knew nothing of vegetarianism, he knew enough about Western eating habits to enjoy watching my discomfort. He tilted his head back and slid the brain into his mouth, downing it in one satisfied gulp, like he was taking a shot. I turned to my own dish. I had been gifted with the creature's tongue, a swollen cylinder lying purple over the teeth like a bruised piece of rubber. I looked from the tongue to the forestier and back to the tongue.

"*Il faut manger,*" said the forestier. "You have to eat. To make the *préfet* happy."

The préfet was the local administrator of the national government, by far the most important man in my village, and I was nervous about offending him. Eating food that's offered to you is a crucial tenet of many African cultures, and the Peace Corps had drilled that into us during training. Since I'd only been living in my village for a few months, I hadn't yet learned to move past those seemingly carved-in-stone commandments and trust my own judgment about when it was OK to breach local culture. So, to make the préfet happy, I managed a few weak bites of meat (carefully avoiding the tongue), then pleaded a full belly and gratefully passed the soup over to the others. Their laughter as they accepted the bowl made me suspect that they had never really expected me to eat it anyway.

The Burkinabè had many customs around food that took time to learn. (I'm just glad that my first attempt at eating spaghetti with my fingers took place far from my village, with no incriminating witnesses.) They also had many sayings. The most common one, which I heard my first day in-country, was the aforementioned, "Il faut manger." To Burkinabè, eating well was synonymous with being wealthy and being happy. They often complimented me on having gained weight, thinking my parents would be pleased to see pictures of me and the increasingly bulging stomach resulting from my all-carbohydrate diet.

Another common saying was, "If there's enough for one, there's enough for two." This could be modified to suit a group of any number. As I biked around the village, if I stopped to greet a few friends who were eating, they would insist that I join them. "Kara, come eat! If there's enough for three, there's enough for four."

Everyone in my village ate outdoors. Houses were used mainly for storage and for sleeping, and even the latter was debatable, since the oppressive heat of the dry season forced most people—including me—outside at night. Being inside at noon was even less bearable. My house had been constructed with bricks of mud and was capped with a tin roof that sucked in heat and trapped it in the darkness of my almost windowless home.

Despite all this, I almost always ate indoors, hiding like a fugitive so visitors wouldn't come across me eating and expect an invitation. At first it was because I was ashamed of my nonexistent cooking skills. Before joining the Peace Corps, cooking spaghetti and heating a jar of Ragu totaled my greatest efforts in the kitchen. In Burkina, it took me months to figure out what to do with a tin of stale tomato paste and a kilogram of bug-infested rice.

Even once I had mastered a few decent dishes, I continued my stealthy habits. Since I didn't have a refrigerator, and the intense heat would spoil any food left out overnight, I always cooked just enough for myself. It was true in African

> *I was thinking like an American, self-conscious about the presentation of my food: the taste, the appearance, the amount.*

families that one more person was always welcome at the table because they cooked massive amounts of food for the evershifting extended families that populated their courtyards. But if you lived alone? I thought their "always-enough-for-one-more" mandate couldn't possibly apply to a courtyard of one, so I would sweat through every meal indoors, then bolt into my courtyard to take relief in the mere 105-degree shade.

Despite—or perhaps because of—this rationalizing, I began to feel guilty about my secretive eating. I felt especially bad about not sharing food with my best friend, Jules. After months of friendship, we had become closer than I had ever expected to get with a Burkinabè. I had listened to his reluctant complaints about the brother who leeched off his dwindling food supply. He spoke to me about the death of his first son and his fears about the mortality of his second. I confided in him about my conflicted feelings toward certain aspects of Burkinabè culture and my growing relationship with another Volunteer. He taught me how to raise chickens, and I introduced him to cheese ravioli. We discussed the existence of God and speculated about what happens after we die.

But our friendship still wasn't enough to break through this cultural barrier. I was thinking like an American, self-conscious about the presentation of my food: the taste, the appearance, the amount. Was the spaghetti overcooked? Was the rice underseasoned? Onions, salt, and tomato paste were the key ingredients that I paired with my carbohydrate staples, and none of my dishes were pretty or tasty. It certainly wasn't guest-quality food, and there wasn't enough to go around anyway.

It was an accidental comment I overheard in the village one day

> *What matters is a willingness to share, ungrudgingly and without hesitation.*

that made me rethink my food-sharing habits. I can't remember where I heard it; all I remember is that the person was discussing a certain meal, one that he had had years ago and recalled with a nostalgic glow.

"Ah, that food," he said, satisfaction quivering on his lips as though the memory itself could bring back the taste. "When you eat like that, *you can even get full.*"

Those are the words that stuck with me. "You can even get full." They shouldn't have been shocking. I had been told during training that some students would come to school without having eaten for two, even three days. I saw the distended bellies and ultra-skinny arms that signaled malnutrition. Some of my teenage students seemed to be just muscle, bone, and gritted determination. Still, the intellectual knowledge that most Burkinabè were undernourished had never quite seeped into the reality of my daily life until then. The realization marked me: being full is a luxury.

That idea percolated in the back of my mind until a few days later, when I was planning to bike to Nouna, a neighboring town about 30 miles away. An hour before I was to leave, I had just finished cooking a yam stew of questionable quality when Jules arrived at my gate. I went outside to greet him, and we sat down in the shaded portion of my courtyard. We exchanged the usual pleasantries—how was the morning, how is your family, how is your wife—and then I paused awkwardly, thinking about the single untouched bowl of soup waiting for me inside.

Then it came unbidden into my mind: *If there's enough for one, there's enough for two.* Suddenly, all the sayings and traditions around food that I had been observing coalesced into something large enough to spur change. I was able to push it all aside: my embarrassment at the meager portions, my worry that he would think it tasted bad, my self-ishness at the thought of biking so far on such little nourishment. What matters is that someone who might not eat all day has something to put in his stomach, I finally realized. And what matters is a willingness to share, ungrudgingly and without hesitation.

My whole way of looking at food shifted. I couldn't take it for granted anymore: food was sustenance; food was life; food was what kept you walking those five miles to your fields, bent over rows of millet in the hot sun.

"Jules," I announced suddenly, standing up, "I want you to eat with me."

"Ah," he said, smiling with a touch of what I recognized as relief. "Bari'a. Bari'a."

When we had spooned the last drops of stew from our bowls, he walked my bike to the edge of the village and sent me off to Nouna. And what I remember, two years later, is not the feeling of a merely half-full belly or the bland taste of my overcooked yams; what I remember are Jules's words: Thank you. Thank you.

Kara Garbe joined the Peace Corps soon after graduating from the University of Virginia and served as a secondary education Volunteer in Burkina Faso from 2001 to 2004. After her return to the U.S., she worked as an AmeriCorps*VISTA volunteer at an education-related nonprofit organization in Washington, D.C.

There is Time

Casey Laycock · Bulgaria

I n the States, I was forever on the go. I never seemed to have enough time. So it was that I found myself in a country with all the time in the world. Since then, I have been confronted with the two phrases that continued to follow me throughout my Peace Corps service: "relax" and "there is time." *Cpokoino* (relax) was the first word my host mother, Cici, spouted as I met her in the stomach-churning craziness of "Meet-Your-Host-Family" day. As trainees and their Bulgarian host families jostled through lines to pick up luggage and medical kits and toss them into rickety, fume-belching Soviet-model cars, I frantically looked around, trying not to get lost in the confusion.

"Cpokoino," Cici reassured me and deftly maneuvered through the crowd like a natural. I felt like a wimp as I watched her effortlessly hoist my huge army duffel bag out of the pile and carry it out to her nephew's sputtering Russian hatchback. I felt even more like a wimp when I found out later that she was a diabetic with kidney problems and blind in one eye. As I ducked into the back seat, I almost felt sick with anxiety and excitement. It was Cici's smile that soothed my nerves.

"Haide," she said. (Let's go.)

"Da," I replied with a nervous smile as her nephew jerked the car to life.

Over rolling hills and past fields of poppies and sunflowers we trudged. Onward, past the edge of the Thracian plains and up into the

Rhodope Mountains to the small mountain village of Bratsigovo. As we rounded the last foothill and looked across the small valley just before the climb to Bratsigovo, with its cobblestone streets, red-tiled clay roofs, and the single, golden-domed Orthodox church, it began to sink in. This was going to be my home for the next three months and the beginning of everything to follow. For a moment, my American "need for speed" disappeared. I wanted time to stop. I wanted to hold this moment like a child might hold a small, shiny bauble.

Cici's house was nestled against the forest. She literally lived on the edge of town, having the last home on the mountainside road that led upwards to the next, even smaller village. Often, I'd look up from my studies to see her returning from a hike, toting bundles of herbs, berries, and flowers; some for herself, some for her neighbors, some for her rabbits, and always, some for me. Always, she'd greet me with a smile as she closed the wooden gate leading to her tiny courtyard. Sitting down next to me at her broken, plastic porch table she'd begin offering me the fresh, ripe berries she'd hiked down the mountain with. Those berries were sweeter than anything I had ever tasted back home. Her smile seemed to say, "It's good, right? I knew you'd like it." She'd laugh like an imp as I butchered attempts to say, "Thank you" and "I like it very much." It was at one of these intimate moments that she told me that she wanted me to hike with her the next day. Like a normal, time-conscientious American, I responded with, in my broken Bulgarian, *"Ako imam vreme."* (If I have time.)

"Of course, of course," she assured me and, without missing a beat, she added, *"Cpokoino, ima vreme."* (Relax, there is time.)

The next day, my fellow trainees and I were told that we had a small language quiz coming up, and it was very important that we prepare. In American-mode, I fervently began to practice my Bulgarian over and over again in Cici's tiny, underground living room. I was so engrossed in my books and notes that I didn't notice Cici standing next to me, grinning over my shoulder.

"Gotova li si?" (Are you ready?)

Due to my classes and studying, I had forgotten our plans and I asked her, "For what?" in bewilderment. She patiently reminded me of the hike. I squirmed, feeling terrible. I didn't have the time that day, but she wouldn't take no for an answer.

"*Ima vreme, vinagi,*" she repeated over and over. (There is always time.)

> *I learned more from her patient tutelage than from all my notes and grammar books.*

I grudgingly slipped into my hiking boots as I thought about the upcoming language test and then headed up the mountain road behind her. I began to chide myself for not being more assertive. I tried to go over my lessons in my head, but as the gravel path got steeper and the foliage became thicker, my mind wandered from the thought of books and notes. On and on we trudged, skirting valleys that revealed all the colors of autumn, past babbling brooks, over the silent, stone remnants of Romanera bridges, and along cobblestone roads with bygone eras etched in their deep, rocky ruts. I found myself standing in a virgin forest on a road that had once led to Rome. My mind reeled at the very idea of it.

It was a sun-ripened plum extended before my face that broke my meditative trance.

"*Yash, yash,*" she grinned and laughed a little. (Eat, eat.) Mortified, I suddenly realized I'd been standing stalk-still in the middle of the stone path with my mouth agape. I took the offered plum as she motioned for me to sit under the shade of the trees that grew at the side of the road. As I munched, I watched her move sprightly from one tree or bush to another, gathering oodles of wild figs, plums, peaches, blackberries, raspberries, strawberries, hazelnuts, and walnuts. When she returned, I asked if we should head home. Cici just smiled, resting her hand on my arm, and said, "*Ima vreme,*" as usual. I sighed and smiled back in agreement as we partook of the small forest feast she had collected.

We continued upwards toward the higher mountain village of Rosovo as we filled our bellies with all of Cici's gatherings. We passed small waterfalls, wild irises, and sunflowers the size of my head. I couldn't believe that this whole other world was virtually in Cici's backyard. On the way, she taught me the words for all the different trees, fruits, nuts, and berries. I was learning without trying. She would wink and smile with every new word I repeated, as if to assure me that I had made a wise decision in coming and that she was much better than any textbook. Of course, she was completely right.

In those first three months, I learned more from her patient tutelage than from all my notes and grammar books. It took every ounce of reserve to steel myself for that final night with Cici and her son Zaprey, who was leaving soon for college. She had made a grand feast of various Bulgarian delicacies as a surprise. She was excited for me that my site was in Varna, the "Big City," but I was reluctant about the change.

In all my time there, I had never seen her upset, nor cry. Every villager who knew I was staying with her would tell me how strong she was, how happy she was all the time. A mountain woman. Yet, that night I saw her strong visage crack just a little. That night I saw her cry. I was another one of her children, she told me, and all her children seemed to be flying away like little birds, but I would always have a place in her heart and her home if I needed. My heart melted. I felt something stick in my throat and tried to suck back the tears creeping into my eyes as I hugged her tight.

"You will come and see me often," she insisted, that mischievous smile creeping across her brown, sun-kissed face.

"If I have time," I said, which caused us both to laugh.

"Ima vreme," she said, finishing our little ritual, her eyes twinkling, "Vinagi." There is time...always.

Casey Laycock served as an environmental Volunteer on the Black Sea coast of Bulgaria with her husband, James, from 2003 to 2005. She received her B.S. in marine biology from Texas A&M University in Galveston and joined the Peace Corps following a career in environmental protection.

¡Que Milagro!

Kerrie A. Resendes · Guatemala

Guatemala City bus terminals were usually my least favorite places. Regardless of how quickly I could move in and out of them, I still hated passing through them. The bus terminals are some of the dirtiest places in the country. Bus regulations are lacking, and as buses make their way through the terminal, they carry the penetrating sounds of rattling diesel engines, continuous blowing of horns, and an indescribable emission of black exhaust. Although, on this particular day, I did not feel rushed or stressed, the stench was there, but not the annoyance; the sounds were deafening, but not overwhelming. In this instant, I recognized that I had become nostalgic for all things Guatemalan. Who could have predicted that even my most disliked places could fill me with a sense of home?

I made my way through the lively terminal to board the bus destined for my former home, San Luis Jilotepeque. It is in the province of Jalapa, located four and a half hours east of Guatemala City and less than two hours from the borders of Honduras and El Salvador. As the bus approached the town, the familiar strong dry heat fell over me. I had not been back to San Luis in more than 16 months.

Unsure of what to expect, the warm hugs and sincere smiles surprised me. Within five minutes of being in my former *pueblo*, I came across countless familiar faces making me feel immediately at home. The women in the market, where I had bought my fresh fruit and veggies, sat in their same spots lazily waving away pesky flies and snacking on fruit. Their faces lit up when they saw me, and they came around from behind their stands to greet me. They asked where I had been, if I had returned to San Luis to make it my lifelong home and, if not, would I take them with me when I returned to the States. I passed by the post office to visit my old friend Mario, the one person I was sure to see every day in the hopes that someone from home had sent me a surprise package full of treats. He took one look at me and exclaimed, *"¡Que Milagro!"* (What a miracle!) Mario said he thought he would never see me again, that I would never fulfill my promise to return. He was delighted to see me, as was the family of Doña Tina, who lived across the street.

When I walked into the *comedor*, one of two restaurants in bustling San Luis, I ran into Doña Tina's oldest daughter, Loyda, and youngest son, Walter. Before I ordered, Walter hopped on his bike and sped home to tell the neighborhood kids I had returned. While eating, I enjoyed glimpses of the children passing by to see if I had really come back or if Walter had fibbed.

In my meanderings through San Luis, I bumped into Don Oscar, the *presidente* of La Lagunilla. He wanted to show me the present state of my woodburning stove project. Luckily, in my 16 months' absence, the government had finally carved a road from the pueblo to his village. I was relieved not to have to hike the hour and a half up the mountain.

To my surprise and delight, the stoves functioned wonderfully and have made a huge impact. The new stoves use one-third the amount of firewood, which has a direct benefit on the environment. Smoke no longer fills homes and women no longer ache from bending over an open fire on the ground. I remember completing the stoves, worrying about whether the metal stove tops would ruin from harsh sun and strong rains since a few stoves were built outside the home. To see houses built around the stoves that were once standing alone in the middle of the courtyard thrilled me, along with the community's sense of pride and satisfaction with the project.

I knew then that my service counted; I felt proud and satisfied.

These feelings did not come from the stove project or any work I had done during my service, but because the community accepted me into its heart. I impacted the people of

> *I knew then that my service counted; I felt proud and satisfied.*

San Luis more than I could ever have imagined; however, their impact on me was far greater. I could never have predicted what my Peace Corps service would be like. Sure, I expected it to be bigger than anything I had ever done before, but I never expected it to provide me with a second home; a place that would become as close to my heart as my hometown; a country as familiar to me as the United States.

As I departed feeling like a town celebrity, I promised the people of San Luis that I would send them copies of pictures I had taken, that no, I would not forget them, and that yes, I would try to fit a few of them into my suitcase. I also promised Mario I would return again soon, even if it meant braving the deafening sounds of the dirty bus terminals.

Kerrie A. Resendes served as a family health Volunteer in Guatemala from 2002 to 2004. She joined the Peace Corps after two years of teaching health and prevention education for at-risk youth in Boston. Upon her return, she began preparing for a degree in naturopathic medicine.

Hummingbirds or Fairies?

Megan Mentrek • Kyrgyzstan

I t was the first of September and word had gotten out. The American was going to be giving English lessons at the community center to the public school kids. For pure entertainment reasons or out of a slim hope that learning some English might be a ticket out of the village, what seemed like the entire population under the age of 18 had turned up at my first lesson at my village's community center.

My Peace Corps assignment was to teach at a boarding school, but after months of being begged on the streets by students of the nearby public school, I decided to offer them a few limited courses during my spare lunch hour. I had not foreseen walking into a room overflowing with students eager to become fluent in English in a few short lessons.

A few days of brutally difficult lessons meant to weed out those hoping for an easy ride whittled the class down to a more manageable size— about 30 students. As I entered the classroom no longer facing the prospect of having to keep more than a hundred students in order, I breathed a sigh of relief.

As my eyes swept the room, my mind finally registered the presence of someone unusual: a middle-aged Russian woman with a shock of bright orange hair. She was with her young daughter. The woman's presence was out of the ordinary because, up to that point, I had had only Kyrgyz students, as I had learned their language to teach at the Kyrgyz boarding school. My Russian was limited to giving directions to taxi drivers and purchasing vegetables at the market. I had planned to use at least a little Kyrgyz in my English instructions to start with my beginner students. How was this Russian student going to learn?

Her name was Natasha, a jack-of-all-trades instructor working as the chemistry, biology, and physics teacher, as well as a stand-in gym instructor when the school headmistress demanded it. Her daughter was Vica, a third-grade student. In time, I would learn that Natasha was once a brilliant student of chemistry and shining star of the Soviet science world, a winner of the honored Gold Medal in Chemistry given to the best student of that subject.

At the time, however, Natasha was more a reminder of my frustrations. After six months of Peace Corps service, I felt no closer to unraveling the mystery of the art of teaching. I could not, for the life of me, figure out how to teach to a multilanguage class or actively engage Natasha as she slipped further behind, solely because of my inability to talk to her.

In her plucky spirit, Natasha and her daughter stuck it out in the class for a month or so, but then quietly stopped coming because they really could not have been getting much out of the lessons. This failing of my teaching weighed heavily on my mind. However, all I could do at the time was to mentally make note to try to right my shortcoming at a later date, when I was less bogged down by work.

The school year flew by, and I still had not come back to Natasha. The opportunity to make it up to her finally came when I had to go to the public high school on an errand during the final exam period. She was there monitoring the door to keep students from loitering and disturbing the test takers. As I walked by and greeted her, I asked her if she and her daughter would like private lessons during the summer vacation. Her face beamed, and she agreed readily so we set up our first lesson for the next week.

When the day arrived, Natasha and her daughter came promptly at the stated time with a bucket full of strawberries. I thought this was a first-time thank-you gift and took it happily as my own garden was under the constant wrath of my host family's chickens and my next-door neighbor's turkeys. Little did I know that I would be kept well-fed until I finished service. Every lesson was accompanied by a gift of food. They could not accept that I would give lessons for free, despite my protests that I could not accept money from them. But I could not say no to regular bowls of raspberries and other delicious produce.

Conversations became more meaningful and personalities started to shine through.

Because my Russian was still so limited, I attempted to get Natasha and her daughter quickly up to a level of English upon which I could base my lessons. This posed an unexpected challenge because I managed to strike about every fragile cord in Natasha's history with typical introductory questions such as: "What's your mother's name?" Many a lesson ended in tears and me trying to console her in my wretched Russian.

Everyone in Kyrgyzstan led an understandably difficult life. The country was not faring well after separation from the Soviet Union in 1991. I had not, however, seen this hard life from the view of Russians themselves. Cut off from Russia, often from their relatives who hadn't stayed behind after independence, and from the lives and usually advanced professions they had once known, theirs was a sorrow I had not yet been exposed to. Natasha was a window into that world.

As the summer progressed and Natasha and Vica picked up more and more, conversations became more meaningful and personalities started to shine through. Because of Natasha's inherent interest in everything scientific, I spent lots of lessons assigning English names to pages and pages of pictures of vegetables, animals, and insects. This was how Vica discovered my phobia of all things remotely resembling grasshoppers. They could send me into panicked flailing that would put most children into hysterics.

So, in one of my most memorable lessons, we sat outside, going through an assignment on daily habits, when Vica screamed out, "Grasshopper! Grasshopper!" She rarely paid much attention to English and

> *How could I break her heart and tell her that my flower box was not, in fact, inhabited by a congregation of fairies?*

mostly came to visit Dunkin, my puppy. After my story of my fear, though, she was sure to remember that word. I, of course, whipped around, ready to run unabashedly in fear. Then I realized that Vica was pointing at something zipping around the flower box by my window. A hummingbird! I decided to use it as a test of animal names. I replied "No, it's not a grasshopper. It's a..." and I started flapping my arms vigorously. She looked at me, perplexed and wagered a guess, "A bird?" I was thrilled that she had remembered and gleefully yelled, "Yes!" punching the air.

Her mother, however, shook her head, and said "No, Megan, there are not birds that small." It was true that it was amazingly small. After working in the Republic of Georgia and in Kyrgyzstan, I found that the hummingbirds of Eurasia are much tinier than their American counterparts and much less colorful. They almost resemble large brown bees. But this was most decidedly a hummingbird based on its flight pattern and obsession with my petunias.

However, Natasha wouldn't buy it, even after I looked up hummingbird in the dictionary. She claimed, "There are not 'hummeeengbirds' in Kyrgyzstan" or anywhere in all of Asia. I did not want to question her in front of her daughter or demean her, as she was the village biology teacher. However, I thought this would be a good lesson for Vica to learn about the amazing flying feats of hummingbirds.

I tried to explain that it was a bird that moved its wings very fast. Vica marveled at this, but her mother persisted. No, it was not and could not be a hummingbird. Vica's eyes got big. If it wasn't a grasshopper or a hummingbird, then she knew the answer. "A fairy! A fairy!" (She had shown me a fairy tale book earlier and quizzed me on all of the words for princesses, princes, evil witches, and magical fairies.) How could I break her heart and tell her that my flower box was not, in fact, inhabited by a congregation of fairies? I left it at that and moved on to try to explain the magic of lightning bugs. Natasha, however, was posed with a challenge. Neither of us would back down on the hummingbird theory.

The next day she returned with a stack of biology books. I thought I was in for another round of what I believed to be unproductive naming of all things vegetable.

I was incorrect. They were books on birds. There, she showed me triumphantly—not one hummingbird listed for Kyrgyzstan. It could not possibly have been a hummingbird. I stood by my story, though. I just knew it was one.

The next day she returned, a little chagrined. "You win," she sighed. I don't know how many hours she had spent the previous evening poring through her old Soviet university textbooks, but she had finally found an answer: hummingbirds flew from Pakistan to Kyrgyzstan to avoid the extreme heat of Pakistani summers. They were not native to Kyrgyzstan, but they did pay us an annual visit.

I felt bad that I had been proven right, until I looked up at her face. She was completely joyful! Then I understood. This was a woman who once had been one of the premier scientists of the Soviet Union, but now was reduced to teaching chemistry and biology in freezing classrooms, with no equipment or textbooks, to students who rarely paid attention. This brief moment had posed a research challenge to her, and she was thrilled! She had learned something and had gotten to argue, and in English to boot!

Vica, on the other hand, was crushed to learn that fairies did not play amongst my petunias. As she had yet to see any solid proof that these so-called "lightning bugs" are truly insects, she was convinced that fairies with glowing rear ends at least frolicked in my back yard in the United States, and that was enough to satisfy her.

The summer continued in a string of lessons brightened by learning on both sides. I would never be able to cure the deepest sorrows of Natasha's and Vica's hearts, but I think I was able to provide a spark of something different. Lessons were a break from the monotony and difficulties of village life, as evidenced by Natasha's words in a recent letter to me, "Your English—it is small light ray in my life." I could not hope to have changed the lives of every village member or to have greatly enhanced their livelihoods in just two years. But I can hope that I was maybe able to sand down some of the rough edges in the difficult lives they lead.

Megan Mentrek served as a secondary education Volunteer in the Kyrgyz Republic from 2002 to 2004. She joined the Peace Corps after studying international development and international relations at Johns Hopkins University. Following her service, she worked educating students in global affairs and leadership skills.

Changing Perspectives

Christina Luongo • Bolivia

hinking back to those first few months of adjusting, I remember the countdown I had going on in my head: *Only 22 more months to go... that's not so long. I love Bolivia!* It was my mantra for survival, which would help pull me out of bed every morning. At the time, it seemed like the days just dragged on. I had yet to find my niche with work, and I wondered if I ever really would. I was just a strange *gringa* (Westerner) in an even stranger land. There were days spent staring at walls. Countless books read during the rainy months. Recipe experimentation to pass the time (by the way, butter-free, eggless cookies are not the best idea). Rehearsing excuses to avoid eating yet another boiled papa (potato) or, even worse, a freeze-dried potato known here as *chuño*. I always needed a daily dose of alone time to decompress and take in the new world around me.

Then one day it all changed. Suddenly, I wasn't the stranger trying to find a place to fit: I was adopted into a family of 137 at the local orphanage. Work, life, and friendship all grew into part of my daily rhythm. Time began to fly by.

And now, as my days in the highlands of Tiraque come to a close, I have been spending every possible moment that I have foregoing the neurotic house cleaning that took up so much time in the beginning so I can hang out with the kids. Where the American in me used to say, "I must be doing something productive," now I don't care if we sit around watch-

> *There was a time when the orphans were just a mix of smiling but nameless faces... . And now I really know these kids.*

ing the clouds pass, as long as some of the children are by my side. I can't remember the last book I've read or the last moment I've had to myself. I only bake when surrounded by tons of little (somewhat clean) hands, and we use whatever ingredients we are lucky enough to come by. I look forward to a plate of boiled papa, or any potato derivation, as long as it is eaten in good company.

One of the oddest experiences I had during the first month in my site was going to the wake for a man I had never met, the brother of the woman who owns the town stationery store. A neighbor took me because she thought it would heighten my cultural understanding. We walked into the front room of the family's home, and right there, elevated on a table, covered in a white sheet, was the figure of a man I had never known, surrounded by neon purple lights and wailing women. We all sat around the body and were served popcorn. It was a surreal experience—more like a night at the movies than a wake from my American perspective.

Three days ago, I revisited that scene. Only this time, instead of an unknown older man, the wake was for one of our boys. Tito, 15 years old, about to enter the fifth grade... and we lost him to suicide. I believe suicide is nothing more than a cry for help, but in a place like Tiraque, people are unaccustomed to asking children how they feel or what they dream of, and cries for help can get lost in the blowing wind.

There was a time when the orphans were just a mix of smiling but nameless faces. When I was so overwhelmed with a new language, new culture, new life, that I couldn't keep a single name straight... and, of course, I was at a disadvantage because, being the only *gringa* around, all of the intimate details of my life (true or untrue) were immediately known by all.

And now I really know these kids. Ana and Mari have shared their adolescent love lives with me while baking thousands of cookies. I am helping Limbert reunite with

> *I've learned to love in a way more profound than I've ever known before.*

his sister for the first time in 10 years. I taught Tae Bo to Hilda, Maritza, and Sulema; Samuel and Daniel taught me to dance *cumbia*. The teenagers and I have discussed professional opportunities and sexual health. We've celebrated birthdays and Christmas. I've given workshops to their families on gender issues and nutrition. We roofed a greenhouse together. We ate freshly harvested fava beans on the dirt floor of a kitchen, staying warm by the heat of the wooden stove. We spent days riding around the *campo* (countryside) in an overcrowded car, playing like a family on a road trip, while Isaac took on the role of family dad. And now we are grieving the death of a loved one.

Every trainee wonders, "What is a typical work schedule like?" That question always makes me smile, because although I had a daily routine, I never really felt as if I was working. Chatting with the women and girls during club meetings, cooking with the kids, making sure their nutritional intake continues to improve—none of that feels like work. There isn't a day when I wake up and wish I could just crawl back into bed again and forego my responsibilities.

The crazy thing about the Peace Corps is, now that everything has fallen into place, it is time to move on. The countdown to the end of my service continues; but now, as I have just three weeks left, instead of wishing the time away, I'm trying to squeeze in every possible second.

These two years and these kids have given me more than I had imagined possible. Even though the Peace Corps had been on my mind since high school, I never conceptualized how it would feel to be at the other end of these 27 months. Tiraque has become a home, the people at the orphanage a part of my family. I've learned to love in a way more profound than I've ever known before—how to be an older sister, a mentor, a friend. These last two years haven't been about work at all; they've been about life, in all its depths, full of laughter and tears.

Christina Luongo served as a nutrition education Volunteer in Bolivia from 2002 to 2004. She then took a third-year position as the education project specialist and spent a year supporting fellow Volunteers and traveling throughout Bolivia. Her plan after the Peace Corps was to pursue a master's degree and work with immigrants in Chicago.

Different Kinds
of Lessons in Moldova

April Simun · *Moldova*

I t's not every year you get a goat for Valentine's Day. My 73-year-old host mom misunderstood a radio broadcast that meant to relay that Americans often give gifts *to their animals* to show their love.

And it's not every day that someone stops you on the road and asks if, by the way, you happen to have any of your hair for sale. I chose to take it as a compliment. And I wondered if she would really want some of my hair if I washed it more often.

But then, this isn't every day.

Gifted goats and hair hustlers are the kinds of things that make life in my 2,000-person Moldovan village zany, crazy, and altogether interesting. (And that's not even to mention the fact that I think the majority of people back home don't really know exactly where I am living these two years. They know I'm in the Peace Corps. And most of them know the name of the country begins with an "M"—Morocco? Malaysia? Mongolia, anyone? But the correct name of Moldova, the little former Soviet state tucked between Ukraine and Romania, may or may not make their Top 10.)

Honestly, I can't say that I grew up my whole life dreaming of someday becoming a Peace Corps Volunteer, and in Moldova, no less. The Peace Corps made me think of places like West Africa or South America. Exotic places with grass huts and sand and excessive heat—even way more humid than in my native South Carolina.

> *In all these lessons,*
> *I'm the student. Yet,*
> *according to my job*
> *description, I'm supposed*
> *to be the teacher.*

But not Moldova. Not a place with unheated, concrete block buildings in the midst of snowy winters.

Still, here I am.

And am I glad I came? You bet.

Because the truth of it is that I can't really imagine any other experience that could teach me the lessons that Peace Corps/Moldova has.

There are the countless buses that never show up—lessons in patience.

There are the many times I make Romanian mistakes in front of classes of laughing children—lessons in humility.

And there are the scrawny bodies of hungry children who don't have mittens to wear in winter—perhaps the hardest lessons, the ones in gratitude and compassion, that still leave me unable to answer the question, "Why?"

In all these lessons, I'm the student. Yet, according to my job description, I'm supposed to be the teacher. The lines get blurry sometimes.

My official job here is to teach English at my village school of 400 students. I teach lessons there five or six days a week to grades 5 to 12. My students are mostly native Romanian speakers, who also speak Russian. But they see English as a key to finding better jobs and better futures.

My unofficial job spans far beyond just teaching English. It involves teaching health—giving information about AIDS, and why patients should demand clean needles at hospitals. It involves teaching about the environment—why littering is bad, why clean water is good, and why Moldovans need to protect their large forests. It involves teaching job skills—how to interview, how to give presentations, and even how to type on our school's old computers on days when the school has electricity.

Yes, the working conditions are tough. The school is old and concrete and not heated. Water is drawn from wells. Electricity may or may not work on any given day.

But with time, you can almost forget all of that. The children are children, after all. And the people are people.

Their stories, for the most part, aren't the kind of stories that make headlines, or that make Moldova known back home. Their stories aren't the stories of revolutions or of loudmouthed, sign-carrying protests. On the contrary, Moldovans often laugh at their own hardworking acceptance of tough conditions.

But their stories are the stories of another type of heroism. Stories of quiet, unrelenting battles for survival, testimony to man's ability to keep on keeping on—through wars, famines, deportations, and economic collapses.

And from time to time, these people with their hardworking, persistent histories stop me on the road as I walk from home to school and from school to home. They stop me to tell me thanks.

They thank me for being here and for teaching their children.

And I thank them for the lessons they have taught me in return.

April Simun served as a Volunteer in Moldova from 2003 to 2005, teaching English as a foreign language. Prior to the Peace Corps, April worked as a newspaper reporter. April says among her interests in joining the Peace Corps was the opportunity to learn about another culture by experiencing it firsthand, which, in turn, would expand her world view and enhance her reporting skills.

The Train Ride Home
Robin Solomon · Kazakhstan

A s my taxi slows to approach the train station, it attracts a crowd of young men who begin to run swiftly behind the car. Even before the taxi stops, they are opening the doors and the trunk to grab my bags. Since I'm traveling light, there aren't enough of my bags to satisfy the small crowd around the car. They begin to argue in sharp bursts of Kazakh as to who will carry my bags to the train. Hastily paying the cab driver, I jump from the car and wrench my bags free from the anxious porters. *"Ni nada!"* (I don't need your help!) I repeat, over and over in answer to their insistent pleas. *"Devushka, 200 tenge*, girl. Let me carry your bags!"* In the end I resort to silence and take my bags myself into the train station. The frenzy of a Kazakhstani train trip has begun, and as I cross through the station doors and free myself from the porters, I have taken only the first small step in the 30-hour journey ahead of me.

As a Peace Corps Volunteer, I'm supposed to travel as the locals do, and in this country four times the size of Texas, the locals go by train, and so must I. With the collapse of the Soviet Union, the fairly well-developed air travel industry also collapsed, and nothing has come about to replace it. So when the need to travel is upon me, I grin and bear it for days at a time, riding the rails.

It's really a lucky opportunity, I think to myself, as I weave my way through the crowds in the station—the grandmothers in their shawls and *valinki* (winter boots), the young merchants with their enormous suitcases strapped to the backs of sweating porters, the teams of football players in matching jogging suits, and everyone bundled up in layers topped with fur coats and hats. Traveling by train lets me see a great deal of this huge country, sparsely populated and filled with seemingly endless expanses of barren landscape. It's a wonder to behold, and a three-hour flight covering the same distance could never impress upon me the vastness of Kazakhstan's uninhabited steppe.

Once past the customs officer who wanted to weigh my pack, I'm onto the platform, filled to capacity with train passengers buying last-minute supplies, families and friends waving tearful farewells to their relatives sitting behind the windows of the train cars, merchants with their hobbled porters hefting unreal-sized suitcases onto the train, and people selling fruit, ice cream, beer, water, bread, fish, and anything else you can think of. The journey to my train car is delayed by people jumping in front of me, insisting I buy their apples or milk.

Having succumbed to the vendors, I arrive at my car with a bag of famous Almaty apples, two *lepyoshka* (flatbread), a bottle of water, and some juicy southern tomatoes. Assuredly handing my ticket to the conductor, I climb onto the train, and I'm immediately greeted by a wall of thick, hot humidity that results from 65 people in an airless rail car for long periods of time. I gasp one last breath of fresh air and push my way into the sweltering car to find my bench. I travel in sleeper cars, as I need to lie down for such a long journey, but I don't go first class, where the sleepers are separated into compartments of four. Instead, I ride in second class, with double the number of beds and triple the number of people, without the privacy of enclosed compartments. I usually choose an upper berth, as the lower sleepers are usually taken over by the people without tickets, who opt to sit on the feet of the ticketed passengers who unfortunately chose the lower berth. On the upper, I don't have to share my space with anybody, but it's pretty cramped.

Shortly after getting on the train, we pull out from the station. The families and friends are still on the platform waving, but the vendors have already moved on to the next departing train. We roll out of Almaty and I settle into my bed for the journey. Outside the window, the city ends and the steppe stretches out on

> *I see the hill that stands above my town, and I know that I'm home.*

both sides. The stops along the way are few, but all as interesting as Almaty, filled with activity and bustle and, most importantly, fresh air.

We roar through some small villages without stopping, and I can't help but wonder what life is like there, in a place with five buildings and nothing else for miles. I am reading a book by a Kyrgyz writer, Chingis Aitmatov, who writes of the Kazakh steppe: "The steppe is vast and man is small. The steppe takes no sides; it doesn't care if you are in trouble or if all is well with you, you have to take the steppe as it is... . Passengers look out from passing trains, shake their heads, and ask: 'God, how can people live here? Nothing but steppe and camels!' " (*The Day Lasts More Than 100 Years*, translated by John French.) As we pass the rolling hills around Chu, the red, rocky landscape around Lake Balkhash, the stretches of uninhabited plains before and after Karaganda, and the birch forests north of Astana, I wonder about life here, and the sedentary Russian settlers who established many of these cities along the train lines they built. The Kazakhs were nomads before the Russians established towns. Sometimes I think that the Kazakhs lived the way this land intended them to. It feels too harsh for permanent settlement. But modernity means staying in one place, even in the frightening emptiness of Kazakhstan's steppe.

On the train, apart from my own thoughts, I climb down from my bunk to squeeze onto the lower berths to drink tea, eat fish and meat, and share conversation with my traveling companions. They are always interested in my accent, and upon learning that I am far from home, they instinctively reach out to me with their Kazakhstani hospitality and offer me a boiled egg, a piece of candy, or some horse sausage. An old Kazakh grandmother hobbles to the wagon conductor to obtain a blanket for me, concerned that I will catch a cold, although I hardly think that's possible on the sweltering train. A funny Kyrgyz man practices his English that he learned in school 30 years earlier. Two young Russian women traveling back home with cheap Central Asian goods tell me why I should come to Russia as soon as possible. After almost two years here, I've learned to enjoy this journey home to my site. The train, with all of its sweaty, noisy, and frustrating inconveniences, gives me an uninterrupted 30-hour reminder of the vastness of this land and the diversity of its people. The train reminds me why I want to be in Kazakhstan.

After 30 hours of traveling, the train pulls into Kokshetau. I know we're coming close because the birch trees line the tracks and there are still traces of snow on the ground. I see the hill that stands above my town, and I know that I'm home. Inevitably, some of my friends are at the station to greet me. They pull me out from among the bustle and crowd and hug me and welcome me back. In one shared breath, they buzz with news of the town since I've been away. I attempt to join the flow of words to tell the tale of my journey, but what I have to tell isn't news. Traveling by train is something they know; it's an old story for them. For me, it's an experience limited to these two years. As I approach the end of my service, I know there are only one or two more such trips ahead of me. And I can imagine that the train rides that I do a fair share of complaining about will be one of the aspects of life in Kazakhstan I miss the most.

Robin Solomon served as a Volunteer in Kokshetau, Kazakhstan from 2001 to 2003, working with teachers, students, and nongovernmental organization leaders to improve access to educational resources in her community. She joined the Peace Corps after graduating from Georgetown University, and went on to become a foreign service officer with the U.S. Department of State.

A Special Meal in Tunisia
Jody Olsen • Tunisia

The sound of the knocker shaped like the hand of Fatima against the carved wood door echoed throughout the house, reverberating against the painted floor and wall tiles in the eight rooms located just inside the Medina in Sousse. Each noon, I knew that sound would take me out of the crowded market with its smells of cumin and ground hot red peppers in burlap sacks and the deep black olives stored in large clear jars, and into the Zinelabedine family's daily life.

My closeness with this special family evolved over time and around their dinner table. I had come to Tunisia as a Volunteer from Utah. My flight to Tunisia was only the second time I had been on a plane. I brought with me the knowledge and experience of the Salt Lake valley with its pioneers, desert mountains, and salty lake, and found myself in a place where the Sahara meets the Mediterranean Sea. Tunisia had known Punics, Carthaginians, Romans, Arabs, Turks, Germans, French—and two world wars. How these peoples and history shaped Tunisia became the center of my conversations with the Zinelabedines.

Mahmoud would answer my knock each day, open the door boldly, and with his loud laughing voice, shout, *"Allsema!"* and then, *"Tafuthal!"* that all-purpose Arabic word that, at this moment, meant "Come in!" He was a very large man, and with his white Tunisian robes, he looked gigantic. That must have been why he commanded total order among his Arabic language lycée students, unlike my chaotic English classes at the

> *Even though I went there every day, each day was different; the Zinelabedines and I seemed to change a little each time as well.*

same school.

Every day our ritual was the same. As we walked up the stairs to the dining room, Mahmoud would describe that day's noon meal and how excited his wife, Suad, was with the meat and vegetables her father had bought that morning. In the house without her *sofsauri* (a veil-like covering), Suad was the gentle center of the lives of her parents, her husband, and her two young children.

The noon meal at the Zinelabedines' was the highlight of my day. The basic was couscous, but the seasons provided variety. One month it might be eggplant, the next zucchini. Zucchini would change to artichoke, which changed to tomatoes. Tomatoes and oranges stayed the longest, and the blood oranges with their vibrant red color almost rivaled the brightness of the tomatoes. The meat truck arrived each morning at seven with freshly butchered animals for the meat shops. The shops would then display the head of the animal featured that day: cow, sheep, goat. Never pig. Customers chose the part of the animal they wanted, and it was butchered on the spot. Suad's father would complete his shopping with something sweet for dessert. My favorite was baklava dripping with honey.

Food shopping ended by 10 a.m., leaving Suad two hours to cook. Couscous steamers, pans, fires, tagines, olive oil, and hot peppers became the core necessities of her delicious meals. Our meal typically would last as long as two hours, and the entire family would be there. Schools closed to ensure that this was a family time. For me, it was a time to listen to stories and to discover a place by the sea, a place in time, a place in people's histories, a place in a world I had known nothing about.

Even though I went there every day, each day was different; the Zinelabedines and I seemed to change a little each time as well. It was very formal at first. Mahmoud would give me a short Arabic lesson and then suggest I stay for the meal. We each had assigned places around the table. Because only Mahmoud spoke French, and I spoke almost no Arabic, the meal was relatively quiet except for his booming voice and laugh as he mixed English, French, and Arabic. Each day a few new Arabic words would join my vocabulary, and with the added words, Suad's smile grew wider and her parents began to enter our conversations.

We talked about why I didn't drink caffeinated coffee or tea or smoke and why they didn't eat pork and why we both didn't drink. I teased Mahmoud about his coffee and his smoking; he teased me about the chamomile tea Suad carefully prepared for me each day. I stopped eating pork.

I brought my stories and family pictures to the table, images of bonfires after sledding down canyon roads in the winter, building forts in the back yard, looking down nervously from the top of a Ferris wheel. I gave them all the stories I had. They gave me their stories, Suad's father's Hajj to Mecca, school in Cairo, the proper way to steam couscous, the way to wear the veil and why it was freeing for Suad to wear one. In our stories I found a respect for differences. We tried not to judge, just discover.

After several months, Mahmoud excitedly told me that Suad and her parents were preparing a very special meal for me later that week. Each day, the family would mention how wonderful this meal was going to be, that it is rarely served because it is so difficult to cook, and how proud they felt to be able to do this for me in honor of my being part of their family.

On the scheduled day, I arrived a few minutes early. Mahmoud's greeting seemed even more gracious and warm. Suad met me at the top of the stairs; her parents and the children were already seated at the table, waiting expectantly. After our usual beginnings, with everyone looking at me, Suad went into the kitchen and proudly brought out the meal they and I had anticipated for so long: a cow's head, perfectly formed, complete, and cut in half.

I knew in the first few seconds, as they all looked at me, that I simply could not eat it. I looked at everyone, groping for words I hoped would

> *And that is when I realized that they would understand; that our time together was much more important than this cow's head. They wouldn't judge me.*

make sense. I suddenly felt out of place. I mentally sought words not in my Arabic vocabulary as I tried to explain that I knew the special meal was probably delicious, but for psychological reasons I could not eat it. I stumbled, I blubbered. And that is when I realized that they would understand; that our time together was much more important than this cow's head. They wouldn't judge me. Suad took me into the kitchen and helped me create a meal of beef chunks, olive oil, and grasslike leaves. I loved it—and loved her for understanding.

When my service was drawing to a close, I dreaded leaving Tunisia, ending my special time with the Zinelabedines. On my last day, the day of goodbye, I gave each of them a small gift, though nothing seemed adequate in thanks for their gift of time with me. I handed Mahmoud a small can of Metrocal, a diet drink, in honor of his size. For nearly two years, we had laughed about his size, my size, indeed, all our differences. Mahmoud put the can in the small refrigerator to drink later. We all knew we would not see each other again.

Fifteen years and occasional letters later, I went back to Tunisia on Peace Corps business. Unexpectedly, I found time to walk through the Medina in Sousse to the Zinelabedine house, not knowing if I would find them. The echo of the knocker against the carved wood door seemed even more hollow to my ears. At last, the door opened, and there was Mahmoud. He was older and thinner, but his "Tafuthal!" suddenly became the most beautiful sound I had ever heard.

After about an hour of conversation with Mahmoud and Suad, Mahmoud stood up, went into the kitchen, opened the refrigerator, and returned, holding the small can of Metrocal I had given him 15 years earlier. He said, "I saved it for you. I knew you would come back."

Dr. Jody K. Olsen was nominated by President George W. Bush and confirmed by the United States Senate in February 2002 to serve as the deputy director of the Peace Corps. She served as a Peace Corps Volunteer in Tunisia from 1966 to 1968, teaching English and developing community health programs. After holding various leadership positions at the Peace Corps, she became executive director for the Council for International Exchange of Scholars and then senior vice president at the Academy for Educational Development. With the Peace Corps, she has traveled to more than 80 countries around the world, advocating for the agency's mission and the work of Volunteers.

Becoming a
Peace Corps Volunteer

Becoming a Peace Corps Volunteer

Since its inception, the Peace Corps has aimed to promote world peace and friendship by:

- Helping the people of interested countries in meeting their need for trained men and women.
- Helping promote a better understanding of Americans on the part of the peoples served.
- Helping promote a better understanding of other peoples on the part of Americans.

One of the goals of the Peace Corps is to help the people of other countries gain a better understanding of Americans and our multicultural society. The agency actively recruits people with a variety of backgrounds and experiences to best share the nation's greatest resource—its people—with the communities where Volunteers serve around the globe. The Peace Corps welcomes people from every background and does not discriminate against anyone because of race, color, national origin, religion, age, sex, disability, political affiliation, sexual orientation, marital status, or union membership.

Visit www.peacecorps.gov or speak to a recuriter at 800.424.8580 for more information.

A Life Inspired—Around the World

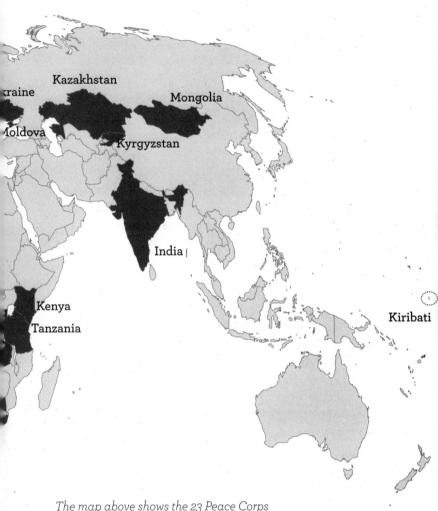

Kazakhstan

Ukraine

Mongolia

Moldova

Kyrgyzstan

India

Kenya

Tanzania

Kiribati

The map above shows the 23 Peace Corps countries—both current and past—in which the Volunteers in these stories served.

This map is not to scale.